Involving Parents

of **Students** With

Special Needs

For my family

25 READY-TO-USE STRATEGIES

Involving Parents
of **Students** With
Special Needs

Jill C. Dardig

Skyhorse Publishing

Skyhorse Publishing books may be purchased in bulk at special discounts for sales promotion, corporate gifts, fund-raising, or educational purposes. Special editions can also be created to specifications. For details, contact the Special Sales Department, Skyhorse Publishing, 307 West 36th Street, 11th Floor, New York, NY 10018 or info@ skyhorsepublishing.com.

Skyhorse® and Skyhorse Publishing® are registered trademarks of Skyhorse Publishing, Inc.®, a Delaware corporation.

Visit our website at www.skyhorsepublishing.com.

10 9 8 7 6 5 4 3 2 1

Library of Congress Cataloging-in-Publication Data is available on file.

Cover design by Lisa Riley

Print ISBN: 978-1-63450-780-6
Ebook ISBN: 978-1-63450-791-2

Printed in the United States of America

Contents

List of Figures

* Intellectual disabilities include mental retardation, cognitive disabilities, and developmental disabilities.

Preface

I have tremendous admiration for teachers. Teaching, whether in general education or special education, is a complex, time-consuming, and difficult job. Teaching has become even more challenging in recent years, as teachers are expected to respond to more complicated laws, changing standards, stricter regulations, and even large-scale societal problems, the unfortunate results of which students may bring with them from home to school.

Yes, teachers face many challenges and have many demands made upon them. First and foremost they are charged with providing effective, evidence-based instruction and with motivating their students to succeed and achieve their highest potential. Teachers are also responsible for helping their students develop positive self-esteem and appropriate socialization skills so that they can function as productive members of society. Given the increasing financial and personal pressures faced by many families, the diversity of the American student population, and often-shrinking education budgets, successfully completing all of these tasks is a tall order.

In addition, teachers juggle a host of time-consuming noninstructional tasks, such as playground duty, fundraising, and supervising study halls, which keep their schools running but their professional plates full to overflowing and their time at a premium.

Additional demands are placed on special educators. Current issues—such as Highly Qualified Teacher status, IDEA 2004 requirements, inclusion, collaboration with general education teachers and related service personnel, alternate assessment, academic versus functional curriculum, assistive technology, managing with and without teacher aides, and new mandates such as Response to Intervention—must be properly addressed.

One important task shared by all teachers is establishing strong communication links with parents and promoting parent involvement in their children's education. Research has shown that parent/family involvement has many positive effects on student performance, so teachers need to make their efforts to get parents involved a high priority. Parents of students with special needs are a valuable but too often untapped resource, and these parents can provide effective home instruction as well as serve as strong allies of teachers who could certainly use additional assistance.

But getting parents of students with special needs actively involved in their children's education is a responsibility that may seem overwhelming to teachers, especially in the hectic early stages of their careers when there are so many new and pressing demands being made on their time.

That's where this book comes in. It provides teachers, whether new or experienced, with a variety of teacher-friendly strategies for establishing good communication and initiating and maintaining productive ongoing parent involvement throughout the school year. General education teachers, especially those who have students with disabilities in their classrooms, will find these strategies useful not only with the parents of students with special needs but with the parents of their typically developing students as well.

I am convinced that all teachers can use a variety of simple but effective strategies for communicating with and involving parents provided they have clear and reasonable mandates and useful models, and they realize that they can construct a comprehensive long-range parent involvement action plan but implement it a few strategies at a time. A gradual implementation process is a good way to make a positive parent-teacher collaboration happen.

But while most practitioners, authors, and researchers would agree that parent involvement is a good thing, many books on the subject merely list parent involvement ideas that teachers must then figure out how to implement. In contrast, this book gives detailed and easy-to-follow directions for creating 25 parent communication and involvement strategies. Each chapter section describes a practical strategy, provides a rationale for its use, offers step-by-step directions for its implementation, and includes sample materials that can be immediately adapted to each teacher's situation. For quick reference, also included are strategy review checklists that briefly list the key steps to implementation. The sample materials for each strategy are varied as to age and grade level of students, type and severity of their disabilities, and instructional situation (e.g., full or partial inclusion, self-contained class, coteaching arrangement, or resource room). By personalizing the samples used in this book, teachers can create their own materials, or they can simply use the samples as resource ideas and then follow the instructions to create a document from scratch.

Additional chapter sections in the book present a collection of tips, guidelines, and suggestions for conducting conferences, making phone calls, sending e-mail, and using voice messaging.

The book is organized as follows:

Chapter 1 provides an introduction to and rationale for parent involvement.

Chapter 2 presents some beginning-of-the-year activities.

Chapters 3 through 5 explain and illustrate group and personalized written communication strategies involving both the classroom and home environments.

Chapter 6 focuses on telephone communication.

Chapter 7 includes strategies for in-person meetings with parents.

Chapter 8 provides suggestions for facilitating and encouraging home learning activities that parents can do with their children.

Chapter 9 addresses a variety of challenges to parent involvement and some possible solutions.

Chapter 10 shows how to organize materials into a parent-involvement portfolio so that you can use, reuse, and adapt these materials in the future. Teachers can also use this portfolio to document their efforts in parent-teacher collaboration, to use as evidence for professional development, and to share with colleagues whom they may be mentoring. Finally, this chapter explains how to develop a parent-involvement action plan.

You will notice that many of the strategies in this book could be considered "low tech," that is, they do not require that teachers have cutting-edge technology skills to accomplish them. Rather they are all strategies that most teachers could use with their present skills and resources. That is not to say that "high-tech" strategies, such as creating teacher Web sites, are not useful, but high-tech strategies are much more complex and could easily be the topic of an entire book. In addition, I believe that teachers can achieve the same goals of parent involvement through less involved, less expensive, and less time-consuming means.

I also want to explain that I have used the term *parent* in this book in an inclusive fashion and intend for it to refer to any adult who is a primary caregiver for a child—including mothers, fathers, grandparents, stepparents, foster parents, and so on, and the full range of family profiles.

Writing this book was an enjoyable task. I interviewed a diverse group of special education teachers, all with at least 5 years of experience and a few with more than 25. These educators teach Grades K–12, in suburban and urban settings, work with students with a wide range of type and severity of disability, and teach in a variety of configurations. They shared with me some wonderful suggestions for promoting parent involvement in general and for conducting successful parent-teacher conferences in particular. These special educators are quoted throughout the text, and their useful materials appear as figures in many chapters.

I also interviewed a number of parents of children with disabilities to solicit their opinions and ideas. I am always impressed with how parents are so often able to respond to challenges and difficult situations with intelligence, creativity, energy, and grace and are able to give generously of their time despite many competing demands. The wise words of these parents (whose names have been changed to preserve confidentiality) influenced many of the ideas and strategies in this book as well.

In addition, I perused a large array of laws, standards, guidelines, and research relating to parent involvement and took the next step of operationalizing these mandates and recommendations into concrete strategies. I'm a practical, hands-on person and welcomed the challenge of translating theory into practice and trying to convert a critical but daunting task for teachers into a doable one.

I have tremendous admiration for teachers, and I hope that this book will help make one part of their responsibilities—facilitating meaningful involvement for parents of students with disabilities—more successful and a lot easier to achieve.

Acknowledgments

Thanks first to former Corwin Press editor Kathleen McLane, who helped me launch this project, which is based on my November–December 2005 article in *Teaching Exceptional Children*, "The McClurg Monthly Magazine and 14 More Practical Ways to Involve Parents." All of the strategies in this article have been included here in greatly expanded form, and 10 more strategies have been added. It has been a pleasure to reconnect and work with Executive Editor Allyson Sharp, whose excellent feedback and suggestions helped bring the project to closure.

My sincere thanks also go to the very helpful, supportive, and professional members of the Skyhorse team: David Chao, Libby Larson, Mary Dang, Mary Tederstrom, and Lisa Riley.

I appreciate special educators Megan Aikey, Tiffany Anderson, Corey Andres, Anna Bayert, Alex Beekman, Vickie Calland, Glenda Crawford, Christy Demetry, Julie Everhart, Goldie Fraley, Tiffany Fulghum, Krista Gavarkavich, Gretchen Gossett, Chris Henry, Melissa Konicki, Monica Kreitz, Amy Leek, Sarah Miller, Terri Musser, Lindsay Reid, Sandie Trask-Tyler, Jennifer Vaughn, April Walsh, Lindsay Williamson, and Mary Zeitler, plus general educator Lynn Heward, for contributing their excellent sample materials and worthwhile reflections to the book.

I also am grateful to the parents who took the time to talk with me and share their experiences and viewpoints.

Thanks to my mother, Evelyn Dardig, for her encouragement, support, and great dinners.

A very special thank-you to my husband, Bill Heward, an expert developmental editor, for his generous and timely assistance even while he was up to his ears in his own writing projects.

Most of the letterhead graphics were obtained from clipart.com, an excellent source of images for use on personalized letterheads and instructional materials.

Finally, thanks to 30-plus years' worth of university students, cooperating teachers, and parents who have shared with me so many creative and practical ideas.

Skyhorse Publishing would like to thank the following for their contributions to the book:

Karen Bridges
Special Education Teacher
Rosemont Forest Elementary School
Virginia Beach, VA

Laura Peterson
Special Education, Grades 3–5
Center School
Stow, MA

Erin Jones
Special Education Teacher
Tea Area Elementary
Tea, SD

About the Author

 **Jill C. Dardig, EdD,** is a professor of education at Ohio Dominican University in Columbus, Ohio, where she has been training intervention specialists (Ohio's term for K–12 special education teachers) for the past 30 years. She teaches a variety of courses, including Parent-Teacher Collaboration, and spends a lot of time in schools supervising student teachers and picking the brains of their cooperating teachers for current trends and challenges, new ideas, and creative solutions. In 1999–2001 she was the first recipient of Ohio Dominican's Booth-Ferris Master Faculty Award.

Dr. Dardig has been active in her state professional organization and has served as president of the Teacher Education Division of the Ohio Federation Council for Exceptional Children.

She worked previously as a curriculum specialist for the Ohio Department of Mental Retardation and Developmental Disabilities, a special education faculty member at Russell Sage College (NY), a research assistant for the Northeast Regional Media Center for the Deaf (MA), and a parent educator for Project Change, an early intervention program, also in Massachusetts.

She has written several books and other publications about and for parents.

Introduction 1

- Parent Involvement Is Important and Up to You!
- Your Personal Philosophy of Parent Involvement

PARENT INVOLVEMENT IS IMPORTANT AND UP TO YOU!

Virtually every contemporary American general and special education law, teacher organization, and parent association stresses the importance of parent involvement in their child's education. Parent involvement can take many forms, such as parents' becoming informed about their child's school program; communicating regularly with teachers; understanding their child's strengths, needs, and progress; helping with homework; attending parent-teacher conferences and other school functions; and volunteering in the classroom.

The critical need to get parents involved is backed by nearly 100 research studies that have found many positive and tangible effects of parent involvement on student success in school. Some of the benefits identified by these studies include better attendance, higher academic achievement, more appropriate social behaviors and attitudes, greater ability to adapt to change, more involvement in extracurricular activities, higher graduation rates, and greater enrollment in postsecondary education. (Henderson & Mapp, 2002).

Conversely, children whose parents are not involved in their education may be placed at a very serious disadvantage, a situation especially damaging for students who are already struggling academically or socially and need additional support.

Although parents of typically developing children face many challenges in raising their sons and daughters in today's complex society, parents of children with disabilities have additional and often longer-term responsibilities necessitated by their children's special needs. These responsibilities may start very early on and continue into their children's adulthood. For this reason, parent involvement may be even

1

more important for parents of children with disabilities to give them ongoing support and help them meet their expanded roles and heightened expectations.

Parent involvement doesn't just happen spontaneously. It takes a systematic and continuous effort on all parts of the educational team, including school administrators, teachers, specialists, and of course parents themselves. Parent involvement doesn't happen all at once, and teachers need to take into consideration the needs, desires, and possible challenges presented by each family. In any case, parent involvement should start at preschool and continue through the high school years.

Teachers are the most important players in this team effort. They can promote parent involvement one step at a time by maintaining regular two-way communication through letters, newsletters, phone calls, e-mail, and meetings; by providing parent-training opportunities such as speakers, home learning resources, print and online references, and "Make-It-Take-It" workshops in which parents leave with instructional materials for use with their children at home; by inviting parents to help out with school tasks at home or to volunteer in the classroom to the extent they are able; by becoming knowledgeable about postschool and community resources and sharing this information; by soliciting information and feedback from parents; and by treating parents as valuable resources and partners in decision making.

This book shows a variety of useful and teacher-friendly strategies for getting parents involved. By the time you have finished reading the book, you should be well on your way to planning and implementing a yearlong—and potentially career-long—program of communicating with and involving parents.

Parent involvement is important, and it is up to you to get the ball rolling and ensure that the parents of your students feel included and welcome to participate in their children's education. Now let's get started!

YOUR PERSONAL PHILOSOPHY OF PARENT INVOLVEMENT

At first glance at this section's title, its contents might seem obvious and straightforward. But before undertaking this important reflective exercise of composing your personal philosophy of parent involvement, let's consider what exactly a philosophy is. What does constructing a personal philosophy of parent involvement entail? And why is it important that each teacher of students with special needs have a personal philosophy of parent involvement?

Dictionaries provide multiple definitions of *philosophy*, two of which work in harmony for the purpose of this activity: (1) "any personal belief about how to live or how to deal with a situation" and (2) "a belief (or system of beliefs) accepted as authoritative by some group or school" (http://wordnet.princeton.edu). Applying these definitions to an educational situation, teachers' personal philosophies should reflect their individual beliefs and values, be compatible with those of a relevant and credible source such as a professional organization, and be applicable to their day-to-day professional responsibilities.

A personal philosophy of parent involvement, then, is a statement of a teacher's individual beliefs about professional responsibilities with respect to the parents of her students. A special educator's parent involvement philosophy will be similar to that of a general education teacher but will include a particular focus on meeting the additional individualized needs of parents of children with special needs.

Why take the time and effort to compose a personal philosophy of parent involvement? Your primary responsibility as a teacher is providing effective instruction to your students, and no doubt you've spent much time reflecting on this role. But you are responsible also for communicating with, interacting with, and supporting parents who share a common goal of nurturing their children and helping them achieve to the highest degree possible, and this responsibility merits serious thought and consideration as well.

Creating your personal philosophy of parent involvement will enable you to reflect and clarify your position on the critical and ongoing task of working with parents, give you a solid basis and framework for taking positive action, and set the tone for your future interactions with parents.

So let's get started by identifying the three key components of your own personal philosophy of parent involvement: (1) the role of parents of students with special needs; (2) your beliefs, values, and role as an educator; and (3) specific parent-involvement strategies.

The Role of Parents of Students With Special Needs

First, consider the many roles and responsibilities of parents of children with disabilities. Certainly there are many commonalities in parenting children both with and without disabilities. But for parents of exceptional children there are several additional or perhaps more intense roles, including the following (adapted from Heward, Dardig, & Rossett, 1979):

- *Teacher*—Students with disabilities often require more practice than their typical peers to learn new skills and more direct and intensive instruction to ensure that their new skills are maintained and used in environments outside of the school. Parents can be key elements in providing this additional instruction. If given the necessary support and materials, many parents can provide important supplementary teaching for their children at home, which will certainly add to gains in their academic, social, communicative, and daily living skills.
- *Behavior Manager*—When a child with special needs is identified with behavior problems at school, these challenging behaviors are often present at home as well. In this case, parents must actively and systematically structure the home environment to reduce inappropriate behavior and teach more adaptive skills.
- *Counselor*—Unfortunately, many students with disabilities face teasing or may not be able to engage in typical activities with their same-age peers. In these cases, parents need to be able to counsel their children, help them cope, encourage friendships, and find appropriate activities in which they can participate.
- *Advocate*—Parents may have to become active advocates for appropriate programs and services, both in school and out, for their child during their school years and beyond.
- *Accessor of Community Resources*—Parents of children with disabilities must often navigate a maze of agencies and programs to locate and obtain community such services as medical treatment, recreational opportunities, and vocational training for their child.

- *Future Planner*—Although the active phase of parenting typically developing children usually wanes when the child enters adulthood, parents of children with disabilities often have lifelong responsibilities to ensure the domestic, social, recreational, vocational, and financial security of their children and must plan accordingly.

You will begin formulating your personal philosophy statement by explaining what you feel are the two or three major roles of the parents of your current students. Your response will be shaped by the age of your students and the types of disabilities and challenges they face. Use the previous list for ideas, and add any additional roles you feel are important.

Your Beliefs, Values, and Role as an Educator

A first step in developing your personal philosophy statement is to read and consider the section of the Council for Exceptional Children's (CEC) *Code of Ethics and Standards for Professional Practice for Special Educators* that relates to the special educator's role in developing parent relationships. CEC is the largest and one of the most highly respected professional organizations in special education. This organization includes 17 divisions focused on the education of students with all types of special needs, including gifts and talents.

> Professionals seek to develop relationships with parents based on mutual respect for their roles in achieving benefits for the exceptional person.
> Special education professionals:
> 1. Develop effective communication with parents, avoiding technical terminology and using the primary language of the home and other modes of communication when appropriate.
> 2. Seek and use parents' knowledge and expertise in planning, conducting, and evaluating special education and related services for persons with exceptionalities.
> 3. Maintain communications between parents and professionals with appropriate respect for privacy and confidentiality.
> 4. Extend opportunities for parent education, utilizing accurate information and professional methods.
> 5. Inform parents of the educational rights of their children and of any proposed or actual practices that violate those rights.
> 6. Recognize and respect cultural diversities that exist in some families with persons with exceptionalities.
> 7. Recognize that the relationship of home and community environmental conditions affects the behavior and outlook of the exceptional person.*

Some important beliefs and values that arise from these professional standards are demonstrating respect, maintaining two-way communication, providing opportunities for parent education, and recognizing diversity.

---

*SOURCE: From the CEC's *Code of Ethics and Standards of Practice* (the entire document can be obtained at the CEC Web site: www.cec.sped.org).

The *National Standards for Parent/Family Involvement*, established by the National Parent Teacher Association (PTA), are another good source for identifying and writing your beliefs, values, and role with regard to parent involvement:

Effective parent involvement programs include activities that are addressed by the following six standards:

I. Communicating—Communication between home and school is regular, two-way, and meaningful.

II. Parenting—Parenting skills are promoted and supported.

III. Student learning—Parents play an integral role in assisting student learning.

IV. Volunteering—Parents are welcome in the school, and their support and assistance are sought.

V. School decision making and advocacy—Parents are full partners in the decisions that affect children and families.

VI. Collaborating with community—Community resources are used to strengthen schools, families, and student learning.*

As you can see, the PTA standards are in sync with the CEC standards and provide some additional specificity that can be helpful in clarifying your beliefs, values, and role.

You may wish to consult some additional sources as well, including any policy statements about parent involvement issued by your school or district or other professional education associations.

In light of reviewing these standards from credible sources, you can now select two or three key areas and summarize your own role as a teacher in helping parents become involved with their child's education and in working with them to address the challenges they may face. Some areas you may wish to include are establishing ongoing channels of communication, listening to parents with empathy and understanding, treating parents as valued team members, providing parents with information about resources that might be of interest to them, and enabling parents to work with their children at home.

Specific Parent Involvement Strategies

Next, identify four to six strategies that you will use with the parents of the students in your class for the current school year. You should list some specific practices, such as sending home a weekly progress report, inviting parents to volunteer in the classroom, and creating a monthly newsletter for them.

Finally, put the three parts (roles of parents of students with special needs, your beliefs, values, and role as an educator, and specific parent involvement strategies) of your statement together, add a brief introduction and conclusion, and you have completed your personal philosophy of parent involvement. Refer to this document periodically as a reminder of your core beliefs and commitments, and feel free to adapt or update it when necessary.

---

*SOURCE: The *National Standards for Parent/Family Involvement* established by the National Parent Teacher Association (PTA).

Throughout this book you will find that many of the strategies described relate to one or more of the statements you have included in your personal philosophy of parent involvement.

Your Personal Philosophy of Parent Involvement Review Checklist

❐ Read and reflect on professional association codes or guidelines (e.g., CEC, National PTA, your own school district).

❐ Explain two to three major roles of parents of students with special needs at your grade level.

❐ Explain two to three of your major beliefs, values, and roles as an educator for communicating with, involving, and supporting parents.

❐ Identify four to six specific parent involvement strategies that you will use during this school year.

❐ Add a brief introduction and conclusion.

Sample Materials

The examples of personal philosophies of parent involvement that follow are influenced not only by individual teachers' perspectives but also by their particular teaching assignments—the age and grade of their students, the types of disabilities experienced by their students, and their particular educational configuration.

For example, the personal philosophy in Figure 1.1 reflects the conviction of a prekindergarten teacher of students with special needs that a strong parent-teacher bond should be established early on. In Figure 1.2, a support teacher of elementary school (Grades 4–6) students with hearing impairments stresses the importance of facilitating communication, social interaction, and community access. In Figure 1.3, a middle school teacher of students who have intellectual disabilities focuses on the importance of home teaching, the use of community resources, and organizing paperwork as the student approaches the transition to high school. Finally, Figure 1.4 illustrates the commitment of a high school teacher of students who have severe disabilities to help parents seamlessly bridge the gap between high school and adult services.

Figure 1.1   Personal Philosophy of Parent Involvement—Prekindergarten Special Needs

Teacher: Karen Chang

Introduction

Parents are their child's first teachers, and even before their child begins preschool they have spent countless hours in this important role. Since early intervention is so critical to the immediate development and future success of a child with special needs, parents and preschool teachers should collaborate to provide intensive and consistent programming in both of the child's daily environments.

The Role of Parents of Students With Special Needs

As mentioned above, teaching is probably the parent's most important role in early childhood. Both formal and informal teaching can address such areas as communication, social, motor, play, and self-care skills. Parents at this early stage should also become aware of the resources in the community in which it would be beneficial for their child to participate. Last, parents need to actively communicate with preschool teachers and other staff members about the needs of their child and family.

My Beliefs, Values, and Role as an Educator

As a preschool teacher who works with young children who have special needs or are at risk, I work with families who are new to the service delivery system and may not know what to expect or be knowledgeable about our program or other programs in the local community. I want to be sure that parents obtain information that will help them make good decisions on behalf of their child.

I also believe that I should provide parents with strategies and materials so they will be able to work with their child at home on Individual Family Service Plan (IFSP) goals and other skills appropriate to the home environment.

Specific Parent Involvement Strategies

Some of my planned activities this year include

- Writing a monthly newsletter to explain different components of our program and highlight community resources.
- Periodically sending home information packets providing background information about specific disabilities.
- Offering several Make-It-Take-It workshops where parents can construct materials for home use with their children.
- Creating a lending library of toys and home learning kits for parents to check out.

Conclusion

By communicating regularly and working together, parents and I will become a team to further the education of their young children.

Figure 1.2   Personal Philosophy of Parent Involvement—Elementary School Hearing Impairments

---

Teacher: Lenore Atkins

Introduction

Parents of children with disabilities face many challenges. Some of these challenges are shared by parents of typically developing children, while others arise from the age or stage of the child and the particulars of his or her disability.

Roles of Parents of Students with Special Needs

I think that the three major roles of the parents of my elementary school students with hearing impairments are to encourage communication by active home teaching, to facilitate social interaction between their child and same-aged peers, and to make sure that access to community resources is optimized.

My Beliefs, Values, and Role as a Special Educator

I want parents to feel that we are all members of the same team, working to provide the best opportunities for their child's growth and development. I feel that it's my responsibility to open the channel of two-way communication and keep parents informed about their child's progress on a regular basis. In addition, I want to be able to provide resources to parents who would like to work with their child at home and in the community.

Specific Parent Involvement Strategies

This school year I have identified a variety of strategies that I will employ:

- I plan to send home a weekly progress report for each student. This report will address not only academic but also social skills and reflect the student's progress in inclusive classes as well as in support-service settings.
- I will also produce a themed newsletter each month that deals with a particular issue of interest to parents and includes descriptions of a variety of community resources that they may want to look into and accommodations they might want to provide.
- I will provide a variety of volunteer opportunities for parents to become involved in my classroom throughout the school year.
- I will carefully document all interactions with parents, making note of any follow-up needed and making sure that this follow-up is completed.
- Last, I will arrange for at least one guest speaker (most likely an adult who is deaf or has hearing impairments) and one Make-It-Take-It workshop each year so that parents can come into school in the evening for a productive and nonthreatening experience.

Conclusion

Though my specific strategies may change over the years, my main commitment to making sure parents are involved in their child's education will remain constant because the benefits of parent involvement are well documented and worth pursuing.

Figure 1.3 Personal Philosophy of Parent Involvement—Middle School Intellectual Disabilities

Teacher: Glenn Hall

Introduction

It's been said that being a good parent is the most important and difficult task we can have, but one for which we are least prepared. Unlike learning to read, do math, play basketball, or play the flute, few of us have formal training in parenting skills, and must rely on observations of other parents in action (including our own), our own experiences, or simply trial and error.

Roles of Parents of Students With Special Needs

Parents of children with special needs have weighty responsibilities to fulfill in order to maximize their children's potential and to make sure that they have the benefit of all their school, community, and the future have to offer. Parents who are not aware of the importance of their roles as teachers may miss the opportunity to help their children acquire adaptive skills at a faster rate and at a higher degree of proficiency. Similarly, parents who are not aware of or able to access community resources may be missing out on opportunities to enrich and expand their children's lives. Finally, parents who do not have a system to organize the paperwork relating to their children's educational and medical histories may end up feeling uninformed, confused, and unclear as to the next steps in their children's development.

My Beliefs, Values, and Role as an Educator

As a teacher of middle school students with mild to moderate intellectual disabilities, I want to be able to help parents work effectively with their children at home to reinforce their in-school learning, find community and other resources that might be appropriate for their children, and create an orderly system for organizing and easily accessing the many documents they have collected over the years. I also feel that communication between parent and teacher is crucial, and I believe that it's my role to establish and maintain ongoing communication with each family.

Specific Parent Involvement Strategies

This year, I plan to implement the following parent communication and involvement strategies:

- Provide a weekly report on each student's progress.
- Send home individualized parent-child instructional practice activities at least once a month.
- Continue to collect information on local community resources and inform parents about these resources on a regular basis.
- Conduct a Make-It-Take-It workshop for parents on creating an educational and medical history notebook and a resource file for their child.
- Continue to publish a newsletter each grading period.
- Arrange for at least one speaker for parents on a topic of interest to be determined.

Conclusion

As a teacher, I try to be sensitive to the needs and desires of parents and to provide opportunities for them to be involved as much as possible. Time and time again I have been pleasantly surprised at and very appreciative of how much time and effort the parents of my students are willing to expend on behalf of their children.

Figure 1.4   Personal Philosophy of Parent Involvement—High School Severe Disabilities

Teacher: Ray Carpenter

Introduction

My high school students with severe and multiple disabilities are almost ready to graduate and enter the adult world. For that reason, my focus with parents is on helping to ensure a smooth transition for them and their children in the vocational, domestic, personal-social, and leisure domains.

The Role of Parents of Students with Special Needs

Parents of teenagers and young adults with special needs face the usual challenges of their children growing up and wanting more independence. For this reason, parents should be aware of the many choices available to their children in areas such as supported living, employment, recreation, and so on and be equipped to counsel them regarding these options. Parents will also need the skills to become active advocates for their children to ensure that they receive the most appropriate services once they leave school.

My Beliefs, Values, and Role as an Educator

I want to establish a personal relationship of mutual respect and trust with each parent so that we can openly discuss any problems that may arise.

I want to provide channels for two-way communication so that I can be responsive to parents' concerns and needs.

I want to become as knowledgeable as possible about postsecondary options in all domains and share this information with parents.

Specific Parent Involvement Strategies

This year, I plan to

- Invite speakers to talk with parents about current issues of interest such as supported living, organized social groups, financial planning, guardianship, and so forth. I will survey parents to see which issues they are most interested in.
- Compile a book of resources that pertain to postsecondary issues and options and make it available to parents.
- Use a weekly progress report to keep parents updated on their child's progress and obtain feedback and suggestions from them.
- Call or e-mail parents of seniors every two to three weeks to see if they have any questions as their child nears graduation.

Conclusion

I hope to establish a partnership with the parents of my students so that they will leave their child's school not only with solid connections into the future but also with the knowledge that they can always contact me after their child's graduation for advice, suggestions, or to share a success or significant milestone.

Getting Started

- Personalized Letterhead (Strategy 1)
- Parent Contact Log (Strategy 2)
- Introductory Letter (Strategy 3)
- Parent Volunteer Invitation (Strategy 4)

STRATEGY 1: PERSONALIZED LETTERHEAD

How much junk mail do you get every week? Do you scan the envelopes for signs of intelligent life and toss out all the rest without opening them? In a given week I receive anywhere from 20 to 50 junk mail items, and they go right into the wastebasket. But on occasion I'll inadvertently throw away an item that I should have read because it blended with the rest of the batch. I hate when that happens, but it's sometimes unavoidable because the important item did not stand out and catch my attention.

Parents also receive lots of print information from their children's schools that have varying degrees of importance. While information from schools hardly qualifies as junk mail, some items that schools send home, such as fundraising solicitations for the purchase of candy, mulch, magazines, or cookies, are not individualized and clearly have less educational importance than notices of upcoming curriculum nights, parent conferences, or changes in school policy, to name a few.

In contrast, when individual teachers send print information home to parents, whether via their child's backpack, pocket, or purse or by surface mail, it virtually always consists of personalized and educationally relevant information. When sending home letters and other materials, you'll want to make these items recognizable to allow parents to quickly identify that the letter is from their child's teacher and warrants their immediate and close attention.

You can facilitate parents' quick and easy recognition of teacher-originated communications by using an attractive personalized letterhead for all of your correspondence to parents. Your letterhead should include your name, school, complete school address, phone number, and e-mail address so that parents who wish to respond to you will not have to search for contact information.

In addition to the contact information, add a simple but distinctive graphic (MS Word's Clip Art, clipart.com, and other programs and Web sites have many free or low-cost selections suitable for use by teachers of prekindergarten through high school) to the letterhead. You can choose a typical school-related icon, such as an apple, notebook, pencil, or school bus, or be creative and choose a graphic that relates to your individuality—perhaps a graphic depicting a hobby such as a chef's hat or tennis racquet or a pet such as a cat or dachshund—and arrange one or more of these symbols above your name and contact information. You could also select an attractive pattern or abstract figure to serve the same purpose. A tastefully designed personalized letterhead will be visually attractive and "invite" parents to read what follows. Use your personalized letterhead for all correspondence with parents.

Some schools prefer that all letters from teachers to parents be written on official school letterhead. In this case, you can simply add your signature graphic and your e-mail address at the top of the page or at the bottom below your signature to give it a more personal feel.

It's a good practice to limit each written correspondence to parents to one page if possible. Take the time to focus your thoughts and craft a clear and concise message.

It is important to alert parents, in your introductory letter (explained later in this chapter) or in person, that you will be sending materials home with their children and that they should ask their child regularly if the teacher has sent any letters home. In addition it's a good idea to suggest to parents of younger children that they check their child's backpack on a daily basis.

Personalized Letterhead Review Checklist

❑ Set up identifying information, including your name, school, complete school address, school phone number, and e-mail address.
❑ Select an appropriate icon, photo, or graphic to identify and personalize your letters.
❑ Use this personalized letterhead on all communications to parents.

Sample Materials

Some of the examples in Figure 2.1 use graphics that reflect the individual teacher's interests (e.g., Mrs. Coolidge is a cat lover, Mr. Hernandez enjoys reading in his spare time, and Ms. Smith loves to travel). Some of the other graphics are more directly aligned with the grade level of the students (e.g., ABCs in elementary school, computer use in middle school, and graduation from high school). Several other teachers selected more generic graphics such as a school building or used a school symbol such as the panther, which is Mr. Pascarelli's high school's mascot.

One other consideration in designing your personalized letterhead is the level of formality or informality with which you are comfortable. While most of the teachers in these samples included their title/preferred form of address, Ron Pascarelli has omitted his title in a more informal approach.

Figure 2.1   Personalized Letterhead—Prekindergarten to High School

Mrs. Betsy Coolidge
Preschool
Street address
City, State ZIP
Phone number and e-mail

Miss J. Z. Wallstein
Middle School
Street address
City, State ZIP
Phone number and e-mail

Mr. Joe Hart
Elementary School—Primary
Street address
City, State ZIP
Phone number and e-mail

Ron Pascarelli
High School
Street address
City, State ZIP
Phone number and e-mail

Mr. Mark Hernandez
Elementary School—Intermediate
Street address
City, State ZIP
Phone number and e-mail

Mrs. Kathy Carter
High School
Street address
City, State ZIP
Phone number and e-mail

Ms. Martha Smith
Middle School
Street address
City, State ZIP
Phone number and e-mail

Ms. Lindy Lockner
Elementary School
Street address
City, State ZIP
Phone number and e-mail

STRATEGY 2: PARENT CONTACT LOG

Teachers should use a parent contact log to record all formal and significant informal contact with parents, including phone calls, e-mail messages, individualized letters, and face-to-face meetings of both the planned and drop-in varieties. Documenting contact with parents is important for several reasons, and many schools now require that teachers keep accurate and up-to-date records of these interactions.

The two most important reasons to keep a detailed but concise record of your contacts with parents are, first, to serve as a reminder throughout the school year to keep the channels of communication open and, second, to help make sure that you follow up on anything you have promised parents you will do. Your parent contact log will help you achieve closure on any unresolved issues that arise involving the parents of your students.

Another important benefit of using a parent contact log is that it provides written documentation of your interactions with parents. This documentation can be especially critical in the occasional cases of disagreements or disputes between home and school. Without this documentation teachers may put themselves and their schools at risk because they may not remember precise details of a situation, including parents' concerns and any actions they may have taken. In today's society accountability is important, and you should assume that many parents are creating a "paper trail" of their own.

I recently spoke with a group of special education teachers to learn about their practices of documenting parent contact. Some of the teachers used some type of log to record their contacts, but several said that they did not follow any consistent procedure for documenting their interactions, although they felt that this practice would be helpful, especially in case of a problem.

As the examples in this section will show, a contact log does not have to be complicated; to the contrary, it should be clearly formatted and easy to complete.

There are three ways to set up your parent contact log—by individual child, with a general class log arranged chronologically, or by type of contact. Each format has its own advantages, and you will need to decide which type of log best meets your needs.

Here are some examples:

• Ms. Soderberg, a resource room teacher, keeps a separate log for each student. She uses a ring binder to store these individual logs on her bookshelf, and she records every parent-teacher interaction as soon as it is planned and immediately after it occurs. At the end of the year, Ms. Soderberg simply places the logs in the students' individual files.

• Mr. O'Ryan uses a general class log for his self-contained class of students with severe and multiple disabilities. He has only six students in his class and finds it easier to record all parent contacts on one master form, sequenced chronologically. His two full-time and one part-time teacher aides use the log to record their interactions with parents as well.

• Ms. Warren, a teacher of high school students with learning disabilities, keeps a telephone log on her desk beside her phone so she can easily record the details of every phone conversation, as it is her practice to call several of her students' parents each afternoon after school to inform them of their child's progress. She keeps records of conferences and items sent home in each student's individual file.

To construct your own parent contact log, make a chart with columns for information, including the date, student's name, parent's name, type of contact (i.e., phone call, letter, e-mail, or meeting), a brief record of the subject of each communication, and a column to indicate if any follow-up is needed. Some teachers use a coding system to indicate the subject of the contact, thereby streamlining this task even more.

Parent Contact Log Review Checklist

❏ Choose a contact log format (by individual student, a general class log recording all contacts for all students arranged chronologically, or by type of contact, such as a phone or e-mail log).
❏ Set up a table with columns for recording applicable information: student's name, parent's name, date, type of contact, initiated by, summary, follow-up needed, etc.
❏ Record contacts as they occur.

Sample Materials

Figure 2.2 shows Mr. White's telephone call log. This teacher keeps two copies of the log—one on his desk at school and the other on his desk at home (because many of his calls from parents come in the evening)—to be sure he records all phone conversations.

In Figure 2.3, Ms. Epstein keeps a log of all types of contacts for each student in their individual school files.

In Figure 2.4, you can see that Ms. Williamson's log is also organized by individual student but uses a different layout from the previous ones.

STRATEGY 3: INTRODUCTORY LETTER

I remember watching a TV game show called *Let's Make a Deal*. Contestants went through a series of negotiations with the host, trying to win as much money and merchandise as possible. In one segment a contestant had to select one of three doors without knowing what was behind it. One door always hid a fabulous prize such as a car, while the two other doors opened to lesser prizes or worthless gag gifts. You could tell from most contestants' faces that the pressure of making a choice and the ensuing surprise caused them not only excitement but also a great deal of anxiety. When their chosen door finally opened some people were lucky and won big, while others were clearly disappointed with the results. Pure chance determined the outcome.

Parents and students are often faced with a similarly unsettling situation at the beginning of the school year. They are excited about the prospect of a new school year but do not know what kind of teacher will be behind the classroom door when they enter for the first time. Will their child have a great year or just average, or worse? Will he like the teacher and be motivated to do his best in the class? Will he feel comfortable enough to ask the teacher for help when needed? Will the teacher be proactive and prevent problems or deal with them before they reach

Figure 2.2 Parent Contact Log—Telephone—Prekindergarten to High School

Telephone Call Log

Teacher: Evan White

2007–2008 School Year

Date	Student	Parent	Initiated by . . .	Summary	Follow-up Needed?

Figure 2.3   Parent Contact Log—Individual Student—Prekindergarten to High School

2005–2006 School Year

Teacher: Ms. Epstein

Student _____ Parent _____

Contact Code: P = Phone Call   M = Meeting   E = E-mail   L = Letter or Note

Date	Type of Contact	Initiated by . . .	Subject Summary	Outcome or Follow-up Needed

crisis proportions? Will the teacher treat parents as valued allies or unfortunate adversaries, or will she disregard them completely?

Parents usually have little or no say in choosing their child's teacher (or teachers)—this selection has been done for them. And if they do not know the teacher ahead of time by personal contact or reputation, the beginning of the school year can be a pretty anxious time. Perhaps their child will be assigned to a superb teacher who is concerned with every student in the class and who values positive ongoing parent-teacher collaboration. But maybe the parent and child will not be quite so lucky, and opening the door on the first day of school will be the start of many months of frustration and concern.

So what can you do to help both students and their parents transition into your class each year as smoothly and pleasantly as possible from Day 1?

A friendly, warm, and informative introductory letter, sent to the parents of your incoming students about two weeks before the start of the school year, is a wonderful way to set a positive tone, allay anxiety, and pave the way for ongoing communication

Figure 2.4   Parent Contact Log—Individual Student—Prekindergarten to High School

Student: Johnny Smith

Teacher: Ms. Williamson 2006–2007

Date	Type (circle)	Regarding	Follow-Up?
	Phone		
	Letter		
	E-mail		
	Conf.		
	Other		
	Phone		
	Letter		
	E-mail		
	Conf.		
	Other		
	Phone		
	Letter		
	E-mail		
	Conf.		
	Other		
	Phone		
	Letter		
	E-mail		
	Conf.		
	Other		
	Phone		
	E-mail		
	Other		
	Phone		
	Letter		
	E-mail		
	Conf.		
	Other		

SOURCE: Contributed by Lindsay Williamson.

and cooperation throughout the school year. Because some schools do not release their class rosters to teachers until a few days before school begins, you may not be able to send your introductory letter until that time, but it is still important to do so, even if your letter arrives sometime during the first week or two of school rather than at the end of the summer break.

An introductory letter opens with a personal touch—a little bit of information about your background, experiences, or interests to share with parents. This personal information imparts a friendly tone to your letter that can help put parents at ease.

The letter should include some basic educational information, such as your goals or expectations for the school year, a list of necessary materials, notification about such details as lunch money, a reminder to look for letters and information that will be sent home in their child's backpack, and perhaps a brief mention of a "hot topic" (to be dealt with more fully at a later time in a newsletter or conference, for example), that is, an important and current issue such as academic content standards, vocational training opportunities, or testing.

The introductory letter might explain briefly how inclusion (a source of great concern to many parents) will be handled and give assurances that you, as the go-to person for their child's experience, will establish regular communication between you and the regular class teacher(s) and ensure that appropriate adaptations and modifications are made for each student.

The letter should express your sincere interest in establishing a cooperative relationship and ongoing parent involvement throughout the school year. In closing, you should mention the best times and methods to contact you for any initial questions or concerns.

A variation of the introductory letter is to send an additional letter containing some of the information suggested earlier directly to each student in your class. If your students have reading skills, write the letter at the reading level appropriate for them and feel free to use pictures, graphics, or rebus-like icons so that nonreading students can "read" part of your letter along with their parents.

Introductory Letter Review Checklist

- ❏ Start with a personal touch (information about you).
- ❏ List some goals or expectations for the year.
- ❏ Include a supplies list if appropriate.
- ❏ Provide details about lunch, buses, etc.
- ❏ Add a reminder to look for notes sent home with students.
- ❏ Insert a brief discussion of a "hot topic."
- ❏ Tell the best times/methods to contact you.
- ❏ End with a warm closing.

Sample Materials

The sample letters that follow not only illustrate the kinds of information that would be appropriate for introductory letters but also model a warm, inviting tone that should help make parents feel comfortable and confident as you set the stage for a great school year. These letters and all the letters that follow in subsequent chapters avoid the use of technical jargon and acronyms with which parents may not be familiar.

In Figure 2.5, Mrs. Poretti, a prekindergarten teacher, opens with some personal information that she links to instructional activities for the school year. She briefly describes an important issue—their new curriculum. She gives information about supplies and buses and discloses her plan to publish a newsletter that parents can opt to receive by e-mail or as a hard copy. Mrs. Poretti closes on a warm and friendly note.

In Figure 2.6, Mrs. George, a veteran teacher of elementary students with mild to moderate intellectual disabilities, similarly links her personal information to the classroom scene. In her letter she deals with inclusion and focuses on an important

Figure 2.5   Introductory Letter—Prekindergarten Special Needs

Mrs. Marge Poretti
School
School address
Phone and e-mail

Dear Parents:

I hope this letter finds you and your children all doing well and looking forward to an exciting school year. I certainly hope you all had a good summer with lots of time for fun and relaxation.

It's been an exciting summer for me. I spent a month in Mexico at a teacher exchange program, working with students in a small preschool near Mexico City. While living with a local host family, I had the opportunity to improve my Spanish skills and learn a lot about Mexican culture, which I hope to be able to share with the students this school year in our "Kids Around the World" unit.

This fall we are introducing a new PreK curriculum for our four- and five-year-olds that we feel will be even more focused and effective in preparing the children for kindergarten and enriching their language and social skills. I will be sending you more information about this curriculum, and we will be going over it in detail at our upcoming Open House. There is a strong parent participation component in this new program, and we hope you will be interested in getting involved in some of the engaging and enriching activities.

The supply list this year includes a box of crayons (a 12-pack is fine), two pencils, two boxes of facial tissue, hand disinfectant, a smock or apron, and a 12-inch ruler. I'll let you know if anything additional is needed as the year progresses.

Please be sure that you check your child's bus number and route (this information has been sent to you separately) and note the designated school drop-off/pick-up points if you transport your child by car.

I am planning to publish a monthly class newsletter this year, along with sending you weekly progress reports about your child. Please let me know at the Open House if you would like a print copy sent home with your child or if you'd prefer that I e-mail these two items. A sheet will be provided at the Open House for you to record this preference along with other information, including the best times to get in touch with you.

Throughout the school year, please feel free to contact me if you have any questions, suggestions, or concerns. You can e-mail me or call the school during lunch (11:30–12:15) or after school (until 4:15). I value close contact with the parents of my students and consider us a team in helping each and every child have a great year.

Sincerely,

Mrs. Marge Poretti

Figure 2.6   Introductory Letter—Elementary School Intellectual Disabilities

Mrs. A. G. George
School
Address
Phone and e-mail

Dear Parents:

It's my twelfth year of teaching, and as usual I can't wait for the new school year to begin. I spent a wonderful summer swimming, camping, and relaxing with my two young daughters but still had the time to take a math methods workshop that has given me many new hands-on strategies to use with my students. I think these strategies will be both engaging and effective in helping the students grasp some fairly difficult math concepts that are part of the fourth-grade curriculum. I'll keep you posted during the year to let you know what strategies we're using so you can ask your children about them and perhaps try them at home.

As some of you whose children have been in my class before know, I have high expectations for all of my students. Because every student is included in general classes for at least one (if not more) of the key subject areas, I work closely with the other fourth-grade teachers to be sure each of my students is getting the appropriate accommodations, keeping up with the work, and displaying positive social behaviors. The students know they can always come to me for help, but I try to challenge them to problem-solve, and often they are able to come up with the correct solutions on their own.

I stress independence and self-reliance and teach students organizational strategies from the first day of school. When students are organized, their day goes so much smoother because they are not wasting time looking for needed materials. They also look and feel competent and blend in more seamlessly in their inclusion classes. To help achieve this goal, it would be so helpful if you would check your child's backpack every evening to make sure that he or she has no loose papers; that every schoolwork paper is inserted into the correct section of the ring binder; that all pencils, pens, erasers, and so forth are in the zippered pencil case; that you have seen any notes I've sent home; and that homework is completed and placed in the homework folder. If items are out of place, please ask your child to put them in the correct place. After a few weeks, this process will probably become automatic, and all you will need to do is check and praise your son or daughter for a job well done.

The supply list is attached to this letter, along with school information about buses, walking, bike riding, lunch money, and other matters.

I am looking forward to meeting you and working with you and your child during this school year. Please feel free to contact me by note, e-mail, or school phone during school hours, and leave a message with the best time for me to call you back if I'm in class when you call. This semester I am reserving Wednesday nights from 7:30 to 9:30 P.M. to receive phone calls at home, so feel free to call me during that time at 222-2222.

I sure hope to see you and your child at the school Open House/Ice Cream Party on Thursday, September 14 at 6:30 P.M.

Sincerely,

Mrs. George

related issue of helping students stay organized. She encourages parents to contact her when necessary and also closes on a positive note.

Ms. Everhart's (a teacher of K–2 students with severe and multiple disabilities) letter in Figure 2.7 is a great example of a friendly and professional introductory letter. She starts with a bit about her background, proceeds to affirm her intent to

Figure 2.7 Introductory Letter—Elementary School Severe Disabilities

Ms. Julie Everhart
School
Address
Phone and e-mail

Dear Parents:

Another school year is upon us! To those of you whose children were in my class last year, welcome back! I'm really looking forward to another great year. To those of you who don't know me, my name is Julie Everhart. This is my second year teaching the primary multiple disabilities class at Wilder. I graduated from Ohio Dominican University and grew up in Columbus. Before attending college to become a special education teacher, I was a teacher's aide in a special needs classroom here in Westerville.

I feel very strongly about communicating with the parents of my students. I welcome your calls, e-mail, and letters with questions, concerns, or ideas. Please feel free to contact me anytime. I believe that if we are not working alongside one another, we might inadvertently undo any progress that the other has made.

You may have noticed that on the supply list for this year I have included a toothbrush, toothpaste, and a hairbrush. I am adding a personal hygiene center to our classroom where students will learn to wash their hands, brush their teeth, and comb their hair as independently as possible. For those students who may not be able to do these tasks independently because of motor needs, it will be a great sensory integration and oral motor activity time for them.

I work very closely with our physical therapist, occupational therapist, speech therapist, and adapted physical education teacher. I feel that my students' therapy goals are extremely important to their overall development. With the help of the therapists, we do a variety of activities and exercises to support those goals in the classroom in addition to their academic goals.

Attached you will find a few permission slips. If you would please sign them and return them with your child the first week of school, I would appreciate it. Also, there are several items that we use frequently in the classroom that are not on the supply list but are on the attached Wish List. If you are able and willing to donate any of these items to the classroom, it would be wonderful.

This year, there is a lot in store for our class. I am hoping to take a trip to Recreation Unlimited (a camp designed for students who have disabilities) again this year. I will have more information about that for you later. I use many hands-on activities and plan on doing several activities with our second-grade peer buddies. I love having student artwork on the walls, so projects may not be sent home right away.

I believe that it is our job to help your children reach their highest potential, and I will work very hard to make that happen. I could not be more excited for this year to start! I am really looking forward to working with you and your children!

Sincerely,

Julie Everhart

SOURCE: Contributed by Julie Everhart.

communicate regularly with parents, discusses a new learning center she has planned, and talks about her teamwork with specialists, as well as upcoming activities. She has included just the right amount of information, presented it clearly, and not overwhelmed parents with too much detailed explanation at the outset. In just one page, Ms. Everhart has communicated to parents her concern for students and her excitement about the upcoming school year.

Figure 2.8   Introductory Letter—Elementary School

Ms. Lynn Heward
School
Address
Phone and e-mail

Dear Parents/Guardians:

It's that time of year again! A new, fun, and exciting school year is here. My name is Lynn Heward, and I will be your child's 2006–2007 second-grade teacher. I'm looking forward to my second year teaching at Great Western Academy. I am a graduate of the early childhood education program at Ohio University and am currently starting work on a master's degree at The Ohio State University to further my knowledge and skills in the field of education.

This summer I have enjoyed relaxing by the pool, spending time with family and friends, and most of all traveling in northern Europe with my family. I look forward to sharing my experiences living and traveling abroad with your children as well as getting to know their special interests. As a special treat, my brother, an English language teacher living in Tokyo, will visit our class in January to teach us many interesting things about Japanese language, daily life, and culture.

As you may know, Great Western Academy has gone through extensive renovations and additions. These improvements will provide students with new opportunities, such as learning music and computer skills, as well as give them a focused environment in which to engage in art, Spanish, library, and physical education. An outdoor playground is in the plans as well and will be a sure crowd-pleaser among students when it is completed this fall. I look forward to starting a new year in our school with all these great new functional areas!

Please be sure to check your child's backpack each day, as I will be sending home letters regarding upcoming events and other items. Also, please send money (for lunch or field trips) as well as personal items in a marked (child's and teacher's name) and sealed envelope.

Be sure to contact me in person (before or after school or by appointment), by e-mail, or by phone with any questions or concerns throughout the year. It is important for us to always be communicating to ensure that your child has an excellent year.

I look forward to meeting you and your child!

Sincerely,

Ms. Lynn Heward

SOURCE: Contributed by Lynn Heward.

Ms. Heward, a second-grade general education teacher, follows a similar format in Figure 2.8, commenting on the school's significant renovations and curricular improvements.

The two final examples (Figures 2.9 and 2.10) show how the format can be adapted to the middle and high school levels.

STRATEGY 4: PARENT VOLUNTEER INVITATION

Mr. Brown is working with seven-year-old Carlo on reading. Mr. Brown encourages Carlo to read quickly and fluently from his book, prompts him to sound out words

Figure 2.9   Introductory Letter—Middle School Emotional or Behavioral Disorders

Mr. Alex Beekman
School
Address
Phone and e-mail

Dear Parents:

It's back to school time! Time for another year of learning, growing, and creating memories. I am looking forward to meeting my new students as well as my returning ones.

I want to tell you a bit about myself. I am a 1999 graduate of Wittenberg University in Springfield, Ohio. I double majored in elementary education and theater, with a minor in secondary education. I have been teaching in the Hilliard City Schools for five years: three as a high school theater teacher and two teaching eighth-grade language arts. I recently returned to school at Ohio Dominican University to obtain my license in teaching students with moderate to intensive educational needs and am so much looking forward to working with these students full-time.

During the first week of school your child will have an active role in creating a personalized class schedule (either written or pictorial) for his or her reference throughout the day. Each day will consist of lessons in reading, writing, listening, speaking, math, grooming, vocational skills, and recreation. Your child will also attend at least one regular education class or experience daily. Needless to say, having a daily schedule to keep all of this straight is very important, and we'll work hard to be sure that every student is as independent as possible in following the daily schedule.

There are many critical goals that we will be striving to reach throughout the year. Many goals relate to the content areas discussed earlier, but we will also focus heavily on learning age-appropriate social skills to use when interacting with peers in our classroom and with the students in their regular education classes. We'll work on conversation skills, manners, and making friends.

In addition, I want to stress the importance of parent-teacher communication. I would like to develop an enduring partnership with you so that together we can ensure the high achievement of your child. Each week you will find a progress reporting form in your child's backpack, and there will be space for you to reply to me with any questions, concerns, or suggestions you might have.

Within the next week I will also send you a supply list, a list of Individual Education Plan (IEP) goals, additional information about working with your child at home, positive discipline ideas, and community recreational resources.

I look forward to working with you and your child. Let's have a great year!

Sincerely,

Alex Beekman

SOURCE: Contributed by Alex Beekman.

he doesn't know at first or has missed, gives him corrective feedback in a clear and pleasant manner, and encourages Carlo's efforts with smiles and nods. Mr. Brown shows interest in the story by asking relevant questions such as "What do you think will happen next?" and gives occasional praise such as "You read that entire page perfectly! You must feel very proud of your improvement!" Impressed by Mr. Brown's teaching skills, I learn that he is neither a teacher nor a teacher's aide. Mr. Brown is the father of Julie, another student in the class, and he comes in once

Figure 2.10 Introductory Letter—High School Severe Disabilities

Ms. Amy Leek
School
Address
Phone and e-mail

Dear Parents:

Welcome to the 2006–2007 school year! My name is Ms. Amy Leek, and I will be your child's teacher this year. I am ready for a school year full of wonderful experiences, and I hope that you and your child are too.

I want to share a little about myself and my teaching experience. I am a graduate of Ohio Dominican University and Columbus State Community College. I have worked with children and adults with disabilities for approximately seven years. I find that teaching children with special needs is intrinsically rewarding to me. When my students learn and work hard I am at my happiest. I hope that you too find their education an exciting and rewarding process.

This school year will be focused on goals and objectives designed for implementation in the community. Your child will be learning job skills and community skills at various jobsites, grocery stores, and recreation and leisure locations. It is my ultimate goal to teach your child the skills necessary to become a thriving and integral part of the community upon graduation.

I believe that parent-teacher collaboration can make a world of a difference for a child with special educational needs. I have an open-door policy for all parents in my classroom. You are free to visit, observe, participate, and see your child learn in my classroom. I believe that communication with parents needs to be informal and frequent, and operate in both directions. I believe that as a parent you are an important decision maker, advocate, and support system for your child, and I wish to include you in all important events, meetings, and changes.

I will send weekly, and sometimes daily, progress reports home with your child to inform you of your child's progress, needs, and other concerns. Also, sometime during the first week, expect to see an information packet about the jobsites that your students will be attending in the community.

I look forward to meeting you during parent-teacher conferences. If you have any questions or concerns or would like to set up an appointment, please call me at the phone number listed above or stop in. My classroom is room 208 on the second floor.

Sincerely,

Amy Leek

SOURCE: Contributed by Amy Leek.

a week for an hour to help the teacher provide additional one-to-one reading instruction and practice to the students.

Ms. Janes, whose grandson is in Mr. Clarence's fifth-grade class, occasionally comes to school to help with art, cooking, and other hands-on learning activities. Ms. Janes's assistance is invaluable because several of the students is this class have fine motor problems arising from cerebral palsy and need individual hand-over-hand prompts from an adult to allow them to fully participate and enjoy the activity.

In Ms. Kenowski's class, two of the dads volunteer in the classroom to help with the winter and spring parties and show up ready, willing, and able to help out however they are needed. These two dads are especially good at organizing outdoor games and making sure that the students focus on each game, follow directions, take turns, and enjoy themselves without getting too boisterous.

Mrs. Marno, who works at a nursery, has donated a variety of plants for students to learn to care for at school and has come to her daughter's high school class to tell the students about some jobs in the landscaping and lawn care fields that they might be interested in applying for in the future.

Middle school teacher Mrs. Crawford's parents do not usually volunteer in her classroom as some of the parents described earlier do, but they do send in treats for special events and donate supplies when needed.

These examples illustrate a few of the many ways parent volunteers can get involved in their children's school program. Some of the activities involve much time and effort on the part of the parent, and some of the most intensive tasks, such as in-class tutoring, require that the teacher train and monitor the parent's participation. Some activities, such as collecting old magazines or cutting out laminated items for a bulletin board, can be done at home, take less time and effort on the part of parents, and require minimal direction on the part of the teacher.

The common element among these parent volunteer activities is that they are all directed toward helping a teacher and students in one particular classroom. Schools often send out letters asking parents to volunteer with schoolwide activities such as a school carnival or fundraising event. These are great ways to get parents involved, but your parent volunteer invitation will focus on those volunteer activities that will benefit the students in your own instructional setting and help build a strong and cooperative parent-teacher connection.

Assess Volunteer Needs

Begin by assessing your classroom volunteer needs for the upcoming school year. You will want to provide opportunities for all levels of involvement, including ones that take into account the hectic schedules, day or night work shifts, and transportation difficulties, among other factors, of the parents of your students. You will also need to keep in mind the logistics of providing in-class volunteer opportunities for parents if your students are involved in full or partially inclusive situations, as you will have to work in conjunction with the regular class teacher over whose schedule you may not have much control.

Typically, parents of elementary school students are more likely to volunteer for in-class jobs; many middle and high school students would rather not have their parents in their classes during their adolescent and young adult years. But these parents of older students can still assist in other ways.

The following examples of parent volunteer activities are roughly organized into low, medium, and high involvement categories, depending on the frequency and duration of the task and the amount of work or preparation required. This list may help you generate your own array of ideas that would be helpful to you and your students.

Low (most can be done at home):

Send in a snack, game, craft, or movie for party

Collect old magazines, clothes, or other materials

Donate supplies or items for a special class project

Cut out items for bulletin boards or learning centers

Care for a class pet over school break

Participate in a telephone tree

Decorate homework folders

Medium (most require some time spent during the day at school or in the community):

Chaperone occasional field trips

Put up or tear down bulletin boards

Help grade papers

Collect instructional materials, such as menus from area restaurants; checking, deposit, and withdrawal slips from different banks; and want ads from several newspapers

Take photos or a video of students during a project

Talk with students about parent's job and other jobs in the same field

Read to students occasionally

Photocopy materials and do other clerical tasks

High (most need to be done at school, are fairly time-consuming, and require some training and supervision):

Help/monitor students using computers

Help with assessments

Provide in-class tutoring—one-to-one and small groups

Serve as a room parent

Adapt/modify toys, equipment, and instructional materials

Share/teach a hobby such as sewing, cooking, stamp collecting, yoga, or chess

Help with the class newsletter

Raise funds for special class materials or projects

Select Varied Opportunities for the Current School Year

Once you have generated your own list, select three or four activities in each of the three categories. Choose activities that you feel will realistically provide most parents with one or more viable choices. Include a total of 8 to 12 choices.

Write the Parent Volunteer Invitation

Now you can write the invitation. Begin by explaining how much parent volunteering can help you and your students, include the "wish list" of the 8 to 12 opportunities you have selected in the form of a checklist for parents to fill out, and be sure to include directions for how the parent can get back to you (e.g., by phone, e-mail, return slip) to indicate what they'd like to do to help.

If you provide a varied continuum of opportunities, you may be surprised by how many parents are willing to volunteer to assist you and your students. If the parent response rate is low, substitute other items and try again later in the school year.

Volunteer Invitation Review Checklist

☐ Assess your classroom volunteer needs for school year.
☐ Select 8 to 12 varied parent volunteer opportunities from the total list, ranging from low-to high-involvement activities.
☐ Write an introduction inviting parents to volunteer and explaining the benefits of doing so.
☐ Arrange the volunteer opportunities in checklist format.
☐ Specify how parents should respond (tear-off form, phone, e-mail, etc.).
☐ Thank parents for their volunteer efforts.

Sample Materials

In Figure 2.11, prekindergarten teacher Mr. Martinez is asking for volunteers primarily during a two-week period when his classroom will be moving to new quarters. Mr. Martinez has listed eight tasks with which he needs assistance. He also lists additional areas where parents can volunteer in the future.

In Figures 2.12 and 2.13, teachers at the elementary and middle school levels have divided a variety of volunteer opportunities into "at home" and "in school" categories in their letters.

In Figure 2.14, high school teacher Mr. Travis asks for parent assistance with a specific instructional unit. Parents can complete these volunteer activities at school, at home, or in the community at either specified times or at the parents' convenience.

Figure 2.11   Parent Volunteer Invitation—Prekindergarten Special Needs

Joe Martinez
School
Address
Phone and e-mail

Dear Parents:

As you know, things are very hectic (but exciting) this year with our new developmental curriculum, our expanded staff, revised assessment system, extensive building renovations, and my upcoming move to a brand-new classroom next month.

As we go through these changes, I would really appreciate any time you could contribute to make these transitions as easy as possible. Some of these tasks could be accomplished during the school day, while others can be done after school in the afternoon or evening.

During the two-week period (most likely February 13–27) that I am scheduled to move, I could use help with the following projects:

- Organize adaptive equipment storage cabinets and shelving—make labels, organize equipment for easy access, etc.
- Assemble crates to house hands-on instructional materials and toys and other items with switches
- Label, catalogue (by subject), and organize the many books I have purchased for the class
- Help with painting wall murals (you don't have to be an artist—just be able to "paint-by-numbers")
- Trim and post bulletin boards and other wall displays
- Set up sand and art tables
- Set up drama corner and puppet stage
- Set up student progress charts

If you are not available or would rather volunteer at another time or in other ways, I always need assistance:

- On our community trips
- With donations of healthful snacks for our celebrations
- By helping create learning centers
- As a reader at "Story Time"

Please let me know by phone or return e-mail if you'd like to help out on one or more of these tasks—be sure to leave your name, what you might be interested in doing, your phone number, and the best time to call if you leave me a phone message.

Many thanks,

Joe Martinez

Figure 2.12   Parent Volunteer Invitation—Elementary School

Sonia Harris and Melba Shaw
School
Address
Phone and e-mails

Dear Parents:

At our recent parent-teacher conferences, many of you offered to volunteer for the benefit of our class when opportunities arise. We so much appreciate your interest in helping out, because your involvement enriches our students in so many ways.

We've compiled a list of tasks for you to look over. Please let us know which one(s) you might consider doing:

At-Home Volunteer Activities:

- Decorate homework folders
- Prepare snack for party
- Cut out bulletin board items
- Take care of guinea pig during a school break
- Solicit stores for contributions (a list of stores and needed items will be provided)
- Check out public library books to lend to class

In-School Activities:

- Chaperone on field or community trip (two trips are scheduled in the next six weeks)
- Assist with Friday morning cooking lessons
- Correct papers
- Tutor one-to-one in reading or math
- Make copies of worksheets
- Supervise students' computer use once or twice a week
- Read aloud to class for 12:45 P.M. story time

Other Ideas? _____

Please check the activities you'd be interested in, fill in the information below, and send this note back to us via your child, and we will contact you soon with more details and to see what we can work out. Thanks for your help!

Sincerely,

Sonia Harris and Melba Shaw

Parent's name _____ Phone number _____

E-mail _____

Figure 2.13   Parent Volunteer Invitation—Middle School

Miss Samantha Adams
School
Address
Phone and e-mail

Dear Parents:

Parents are always welcome in our school and in my classroom, and I want to offer a variety of opportunities for you to get involved.

I would so much appreciate help with the following tasks. If you could assist with one or more of them, just let me know by checking the items you're interested in and tearing off the form and sending it back to me. I'll be in touch soon to work out the details.

Many thanks,

Samantha Adams

Cut here --

At-Home Volunteer Activities:	Check if Interested
Label/organize individual student prep folders	
Cut out laminated materials for learning centers	
Start seeds for gardening/plant care unit	
Contribute grooming items, such as soap, toothbrushes, combs, a large mirror, etc.	
Contribute easy-to-prepare recipes—written on 5″ × 7″ index cards	
Call or visit stores for contributions of items as needed	
Other ideas?	

In-School Volunteer Activities:	Check if Interested
Accompany us on trips to Statehouse and/or City Hall (February 24 and April 5, respectively)	
Assist with Wednesday morning social skills lessons (10:00–10:45 A.M.)	
Tutor one-to-one in reading or math (one hour or more weekly)	
Participate in mock job interviews (sometime in November)	
Create filing system for worksheets, learning centers, folder games, etc. (anytime you're available)	
Talk to students about your career and job opportunities in your field (time to be arranged at your convenience)	
Other ideas?	

Parent's name_____ Phone number _____ E-mail _____

Figure 2.14   Parent Volunteer Invitation—High School Severe Disabilities

Mr. J. Travis
School
Address
Phone and e-mail

Dear Parents:

The school year is going well, and I wanted to let you know about a special unit we're starting and to ask for your help in making it a valuable experience for all of our students.

Because most of the students in our class are within two or three years of graduation and independent or supported living is a long-range goal for most of our students and their families, we are embarking on our "Apartment Hunting" unit. Some of the skills included in the unit are assessing one's community living needs, reading the classified ads, and evaluating apartments for suitability and desirability.

After completing the school-based parts of this unit we will be taking several trips into the community so that students can individually evaluate apartments in relation to their own identified needs. This is where I need your assistance. I am looking for parents who are willing to accompany us on one or more of these trips and provide one-to-one assistance to students (not your own child, however) as they complete their "Apartment Evaluation Checklists." On the day of each trip, I would ask that each parent join me for lunch at school (my treat) at 11:30 so I can brief you on the procedure and strategies I'd like you to follow. Then we'll leave with the students via school van at 12:15 and return to school by 3:15. The trips are scheduled for Monday, April 6; Wednesday, April 15; and Thursday, April 16.

There are several other volunteer opportunities for this instructional unit if you are not able to accompany us into the community during the day. These opportunities are listed below, and I will provide more details for each choice if you indicate interest.

Please tear off and send the checklist below back to school with your child, and don't worry if you are not able to participate at this time. There will be more opportunities in the future!

Thanks,

James Travis

Cut here --

I will be able to (or want more information about):

- Go on field trip Monday, April 6
- Go on field trip Wednesday, April 15
- Go on field trip Thursday, April 16
- Take digital photos on field trip(s)
- Collect classified ads from local newspapers
- Come to school to laminate ads and prepare interactive folders
- Take digital photos of apartment complexes in the area
- Stop by area apartment complexes and collect information about floor plans, amenities, leases, etc.

Your name _____

Phone number and/or e-mail _____

Designing Your Classroom to Educate Parents

- The Visible Curriculum (Strategy 5)

STRATEGY 5: THE VISIBLE CURRICULUM

School curriculum is made up of two components. First and foremost is the academic (or functional in the case of students with severe disabilities) curriculum that covers key subjects, such as language arts, math, social studies, and science, plus physical, health, technology, and arts education. In the past decade, state-mandated academic content standards have made a critical impact on PreK–12 classroom instruction, and most Individual Education Plans (IEPs), in whole or in part, are derived from or at least referenced to the same standards addressed in the general education curriculum.

The second component of curriculum—the social/behavioral curriculum—is less standardized and often receives much less attention than the academic component. However, for many students with special needs the social/behavioral curriculum is as important as the academic, and many IEPs include social/behavioral objectives as well as academic ones. In this area, most teachers establish a set of classroom rules that students must follow. These rules should be explicitly and clearly stated so that students, whether at the elementary or high school levels or in self-contained or inclusive settings, know the rules and the consequences for following or breaking them.

Parents should have a clear understanding of the entire school curriculum as it affects their child, including both academic objectives and the school's and teachers' social/behavioral expectations for students. If parents are made aware of academic standards they will be better able to work with their children at home on targeted objectives in reading, math, writing, and other subjects. Similarly, if parents are made aware of classroom rules, they can encourage their children to follow them and can even give their children extended and consistent practice at home in skills such as taking turns, being punctual, getting prepared, staying organized, speaking respectfully to others, and taking care of property. These social behaviors will be important in postsecondary education and later on when students transition into employment and need, in addition to being skilled and capable employees, to blend in socially with their peers in the workplace.

Parents may visit your classroom on many occasions, both formal (such as for conferences and to volunteer) and informal (such as picking up their child for a doctor's appointment or delivering a forgotten lunchbox), throughout the school year. These visits can double as opportunities for parents to learn what's going on in both the academic and social/behavioral sides of the curriculum if you use your classroom walls to make the curriculum visible to parents when they enter your classroom.

Two Posters

Create a visible curriculum by making two posters. The first poster lists the grade level academic standards (either "as is" or modified) and/or functional skill objectives targeted for your students. A movable visual marker (such as a clothespin or arrow attached by hook-and-loop tape) can indicate which specific standards or objectives are being worked on at any given time. The second poster explains class rules for student behavior and can be posted beside the one displaying academic standards to give parents a view of the social skills their child is learning. These two posters inform parents (as well as the students, other staff members, and volunteers) about the curriculum every time they enter the classroom.

As a special educator, how could you implement a visible curriculum when your students are included in general education classrooms for most or all of the school day? If you have only a small space or you don't even have a room of your own, see if you can find a nearby bulletin board to post this important information for parents, or ask the general education teachers if you can display the posters in their classrooms. Information about the curriculum will be of interest to parents of typically developing students as well.

Of course, not every parent will read the information you've taken the time to prepare and post. That's why it's also important to present this information to parents during open school nights, curriculum nights, and parent conferences.

Visible Curriculum Review Checklist

☐ Identify targeted academic content standards and/or functional skills/objectives.
☐ Create a poster listing these skills/objectives.
☐ Obtain a movable marker.
☐ Identify class rules or work with your class to develop them.
☐ Create a poster with class rules.
☐ Hang up both posters in your classroom or another area where parents are likely to see them.

Sample Materials

Figures 3.1–3.3 illustrate posters of state academic content standards in world history, language arts, mathematics, and social studies at various grade levels. The posters use various layouts and markers (clips, self-adhesive notes, a circular spinner, arrows, etc.) to indicate the goals currently being worked on.

Figure 3.1   Visible Curriculum, Academic: Language Arts—Middle School

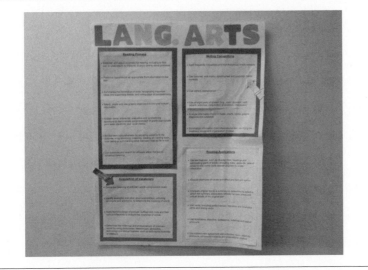

SOURCE: Contributed by Gretchen Gossett.

Visible Curriculum, Academic: World History—High School

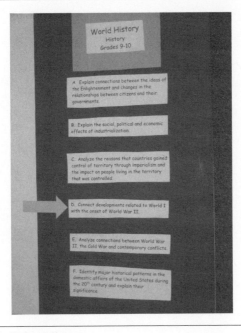

SOURCE: Contributed by Hayley McClaine.

Figure 3.2   Visible Curriculum, Academic: Language Arts—Middle School

SOURCE: Contributed by Megan Aikey.

Visible Curriculum, Academic: Math—Middle School

SOURCE: Contributed by Tiffany Fulghum.

Figure 3.3   Visible Curriculum, Academic: Math—Elementary School

SOURCE: Contributed by Tiffany Anderson.

Visible Curriculum, Academic: Social Studies—Elementary School

SOURCE: Contributed by Alex Beekman.

The boxes in Figure 3.4 show examples of posted rules at three grade levels (prekindergarten, elementary, and middle school) that parents can view in your classroom. They then can reinforce some of the same appropriate behaviors (such as speaking quietly and politely, putting away belongings, and helping others) at home.

Figure 3.4   Visible Curriculum, Social/Behavioral—Prekindergarten to Middle School

---

Class Rules (Prekindergarten)

Hang your coat on your peg.

Put your lunch in the lunch bin.

Wait for your turn to line up or play a game.

Put toys and books back when you are finished with them.

Speak nicely to teachers and students.

Keep your hands to yourself.

Be a good friend to students who have wheelchairs or walkers and need your help.

Class Rules (Elementary School)

Listen when others are talking.

Follow directions.

Keep hands, feet, and objects to yourself (in your own space).

Work quietly without making sounds (so you don't disturb others).

Raise your hand before speaking.

Show respect for school and personal property.

Work and play in a safe manner.

SOURCE: Contributed by Lynn Heward.

Class Rules (Elementary School)

Come to class ready to work.

Speak respectfully to others.

Follow the teacher's directions.

Keep your property on or inside your desk.

Get your materials ready quickly when it's time to work.

Ask permission to go to restroom or get a drink and be sure to take a pass.

Volunteer to assist a classmate who needs help.

Check your mailbox before you go home.

Class Rules (Middle School)

Come to class on time.

Sit in your assigned seat.

Put your homework in the "Homework Inbox."

Take out a pen and a notebook and any other materials for today's lesson.

Participate in discussions, but raise your hand when you want to speak.

Speak quietly and politely.

Make responsible choices.

Group Written Communication and Interaction

- Suggestion Box Letter (Strategy 6)
- Class Newsletter (Strategy 7)

STRATEGY 6: SUGGESTION BOX LETTER

Many years ago I worked for a large cookie company that supplied employees with pencils printed with the phrase "Think and Suggest" on the side. There was a suggestion box in each office, and we were encouraged to come up with ideas to improve or streamline our operations. Quite a few employees made suggestions so helpful that they saved the company thousands of dollars. These suggestions from frontline employees were most meaningful because of their contributors' day-to-day practical experience coupled with a strong motivation to make their jobs easier and to improve the overall position of the company.

Parents, like employees, are on the front lines as well and can be a great source of suggestions for classroom improvements. A teacher who periodically sends parents a letter asking them to contribute suggestions may acquire some useful ideas and demonstrate to parents in a tangible way that their opinions are of value.

Suggestions can be specific to one parent's child or can apply to the general class operation or routine. The following examples illustrate both of these types of suggestions sent in by parents:

- Please move Marcy away from the window to a front row. She gives me daily detailed accounts of cars and people going in and out of the parking lot that make me think she's getting distracted and not paying attention where she should.

- I suggest that you ask parents to send in old shirts or aprons to use when you have a cooking lesson or another messy activity. I can contribute six aprons if you want them.
- How about using actual local restaurant menus to supplement those in the workbook the students are bringing home? If you like, I can collect some menus when we eat out and send them in to school.
- Could you send home any resources that deal with how to help kids with homework? I have talked with several other parents who are also having problems with this issue.
- Please remind Jack to check his backpack every afternoon before getting on the bus to be sure all his homework materials are in there. Please place any notes you send home in the outside pocket of his backpack so we don't have to search for them. Thanks!
- It would be so helpful if you would check with the regular education teachers and notify parents a week or two before unit tests or big projects are due in the students' inclusive classrooms.
- Consider moving student mailboxes nearer to the exit door so parents don't need to walk through class and create a distraction when picking up students in the afternoon.

Many of the suggestions you will receive from parents will be useful and fairly easy to implement. Some suggestions may not be feasible or even desirable. In any case, always follow up with parents who send in suggestions to thank them and tell them how you implemented their idea—or if not, why.

Suggestion Box Letter Review Checklist

- ❏ Write an opening paragraph inviting parent suggestions.
- ❏ Set up the format for parent response.
- ❏ Specify how parents should respond (tear-off form, phone, e-mail, etc.).
- ❏ Be sure to report back to parents on suggestions, whether used or not.

Sample Materials

Ms. Walsh's suggestion box letter (Figure 4.1) to parents of elementary students provides a general, attractive, but simple form to fill in with suggestions in specific areas with which a parent is concerned, while middle school teacher Ms. Walstein's form (Figure 4.2) is a little more open ended. Mr. Banks's letter (Figure 4.3) to parents of middle school students breaks down the suggestion box form into four sections to focus responses on the particular areas where he would like ideas. High school teacher Ms. Endo's letter (Figure 4.4) asks for suggestions pertaining to a specific curricular area—nutrition and cooking.

Figure 4.1 Suggestion Box Letter—Elementary School

Ms. April Walsh
School
Address
Phone and e-mail

Hello, Parents!

As you know, parents are one of the most important factors in their child's success at school, and I have found that parents can be wonderful resources for me as well, as we progress through the school year. With that said, I am sending you this "Suggestion Box" letter to increase your direct impact on your student's experiences in the school environment. Please take a few moments to reflect upon your student's progress so far and jot down any suggestions that you think might be helpful.

Below I have attached a tear-off sheet that you may return to me in your student's bag. Please consider each area and share any ideas that come to mind.

If you do have suggestions, simply complete the form and return it to me. There is no deadline for these suggestions, so feel free to send it in whenever you come up with ideas you'd like to share. When you return one sheet, I will slip another into your son/daughter's bag so you can make suggestions whenever you want. Feel free to leave your name in the space provided so that I can get back to you on the progress of your suggestion. If you don't wish to leave your name, that's fine too.

I have been so impressed with your involvement thus far and anticipate bettering our school life with your suggestions!

Thanks again,
April Walsh

MS. WALSH'S "SUGGESTION BOX"

Parent's name (optional) _____

Date _____

IEP goal activities		Daily living skills	
Community trips		Art/Music/Adapted physical education	
Group activities		Vocational goals	
Leisure activities		Other	

SOURCE: Contributed by April Walsh.

Figure 4.2   Suggestion Box Letter—Middle School

Wendy Walstein
School
Address
Phone and e-mail

Dear Parents:

Like many of my colleagues, during the school year I regularly take the time to reflect upon how things are going. Of course, I take pride in my students' accomplishments, but I also attempt to identify areas that need attention, and I try to be creative about coming up with solutions. Along with self-reflection, I actively seek suggestions from other teachers, in both special and general education, and from specialists about how to improve the teaching/learning process and the classroom environment.

As we're already well into the school year, and I know you are familiar with many aspects of my classroom and the curriculum, I would appreciate your taking a minute to jot down any suggestions you might have that would enhance our educational environment in any way. I can't promise that all of your suggestions will be followed, but I will read and consider each one carefully and respond back to you whether or not the suggestion is implemented.

If you wish to share an idea for my "Suggestion Box," please fill out and tear off the attached form and send it back to me with your student, by surface mail, or via e-mail.

Many thanks,

Wendy Walstein

SUGGESTION BOX IDEA FROM PARENT:

I suggest that you consider trying the following:

_____

_____

_____

_____

_____

because _____

_____

_____

_____

Parent's name: _____

Parent's phone number and/or e-mail _____

Please return this response form to Ms. Walstein.

Figure 4.3   Suggestion Box Letter—Middle School Intellectual Disabilities

Mr. Joseph Banks
School
Address
Phone and e-mail

Attention Parents: Please contribute an idea to my Suggestion Box!

Dear Parents:

Each grading period I will be asking you to contribute any suggestions you might have on ways to improve my class. In the past, parents have been a wonderful source of ideas for me, and I am hoping that you will be willing to share your thoughts with me this year as well.

Please fill in your ideas in the chart below and return this form to me. If you include your name, I would be happy to get back to you to let you know if I have been able to follow your suggestion.

Thanks!
Joe Banks

Suggestions about the classroom:
Suggestions about our curriculum, methods, or materials:
Suggestions concerning your child: Child's name:_____
Other ideas:

Your name (optional) _____

Figure 4.4   Suggestion Box Letter—High School Severe Disabilities

Ms. Miyoko Endo
School
Address
Phone and e-mail

Dear Parents:

This year I am planning several nutrition and cooking units for my class. All of the students seem to be very interested in learning how to plan meals for themselves and their friends and families. This is very good news because it's so important for high school students to be able to plan and prepare healthful snacks and meals and to be as independent as possible in the kitchen. These food preparation units also allow us to work on social interaction skills, such as good table manners and appropriate conversation with peers, as well as skills in math, reading, and following multistep directions.

I am looking for suggestions for your family's favorite snacks and easy-to-make dishes that we could learn to prepare in class. I am especially interested in one-dish meals such as casseroles, salads, or stews.

Please fill out this tear-off form that you can send back to me via your son or daughter, and include any recipes that you'd like to suggest. Being a pretty good cook myself, I can usually adapt somewhat complicated recipes, and I always send home with the students simplified and picture recipes that I use in class. Thanks to the generosity of parents, we also have a very good supply of kitchen equipment so that all students can complete each step of a recipe as we prepare it.

Thanks in advance for your suggestions!

Miyoko Endo

Cut here ---

Your name _____

Your Family's **Favorite Snacks:**

Snack Name	Recipe Attached?

Your Family's **Favorite Dishes** (especially one-dish meals):

Dish Name	Recipe Attached?

Your Student's **Favorite Ingredients:**

Please return this form to Ms. Endo.

STRATEGY 7: CLASS NEWSLETTER

Imagine for a moment that you are the parent of Jake, a child with special needs. Perhaps Jake lets you know one or two things he did at school on a particular day but is not able to articulate or is not skilled at giving you any additional information about what's going on in his classroom, resource room, or inclusive situation. Although you would like to visit Jake's class to see for yourself and get the "big picture," you have a full-time job, other children at home, or demands on your time that prevent you from doing so.

But every month when you receive a newsletter from Jake's teacher, you sit down with a cup of coffee and spend 5–10 minutes reading interesting news and helpful suggestions and just getting the feel of the place where your child spends six hours a day, five days a week, nine months a year. It's time well spent, because you can talk about the news in the articles you've read, you can make a note to be sure your child is prepared for upcoming activities, and you may even get a few ideas about home learning activities to try. You welcome news not only about Jake but also about his class and peers. You feel in touch with what's going on and appreciate this periodic glimpse into Jake's day-to-day educational world, courtesy of your child's teacher.

The Teacher's Perspective

A class newsletter sounds great from the parent's point of view. But as the teacher charged with actually creating the newsletter, your point of view may be a little different. You are busy with students, meetings, class preparations, and collaborating with other teachers and specialists, duties, and paperwork, and the idea of creating a class newsletter may seem like a task that would require more time and attention than you can spare. But by investing a little creative energy up front to design a format for your class newsletter and then following the same pattern for each new issue, you will find that it is relatively easy to use this functional and engaging vehicle to communicate with your students' families on a regular basis.

Newsletter Contents

Your newsletter should feature information about your own class (or classes) and students rather than about an entire grade or school. In the first issue you'll want to provide an interesting mix of items—perhaps five to six articles total. Article topics might include the following:

- *Our Trip to See "The Story of Rosa Parks."* A successful past activity (or one in progress) such as a themed instructional unit, field trip, or ongoing curricular area
- *April Unit: The Power of Tornadoes.* Future plans for an upcoming instructional unit
- *Three Cheers for Laura.* Good news about individual students—an academic or functional skill accomplishment, award, or a bit of interesting personal news (e.g., a new sibling, unusual vacation)
- *Meet Mr. Gonzales, Our Physical Therapist.* A profile of a specialist (e.g., an occupational or speech therapist, librarian, or adapted physical education teacher) or a general education class teacher. Tell a little about the individual and what he or she does for your students.
- *Ms. Marshall Says "Welcome to the Library!"* An article from a guest columnist (one of the specialists or teachers mentioned earlier)

- *Great Web Site of the Month.* Notice of useful resources (books, Web sites, summer camp directories, etc.) or opportunities (volunteer, local meetings, etc.) of special interest to parents
- *We Need Your Old Magazines.* A request for parents to send in any items or materials that your students might need
- *Simple Snacks Your Child Can Prepare at Home.* Suggestions for home activities that reinforce, enrich, or extend skills that you are working on in class
- *Question of the Month: How Can I Help My Teen Get an Afterschool Job?* A question posed by a parent (not identified by name) and your thoughtful response
- *Using Photos to Help Your Child Choose From a Menu.* Adaptations and modifications to home and community activities that parents can do to increase their child's active participation
- *We Love Our New Boardmaker!* A description of a new piece of adaptive equipment, software, or great instructional material you have acquired for the class
- *Stuck in an Elevator.* A "thought piece" in which you recount a significant in- or out-of-school anecdote (no names here either) and your reflection on it

Keep the articles brief (about 75–250 words each in most cases) and the writing informal, clear, interesting, to the point, and in the first person. Proofread your class newsletter carefully to be sure it is free of spelling, grammar, and punctuation errors.

Newsletter Format and Design

You don't have to be a graphic artist to design a newsletter, and by using some of the following suggestions you will be able to create an attractive publication that parents will enjoy reading.

Although many commercial newsletter templates or wizards are available for purchase and even some that you can download free from the Internet, you can easily create a newsletter on your computer by using Microsoft Word and its many helpful features (or any writing program for that matter).

Start at the top of the page by identifying your class newsletter—choose a title and be sure to include your name, class, school, school phone number, your e-mail address, and the date of the issue. Use the graphic you have chosen for your personalized letterhead on the newsletter heading to visually link this publication to you so parents will immediately recognize that the newsletter is a communication from their child's teacher and not a general school publication.

Use short headlines (such as the ones used in the previous list of topic suggestions) to highlight each article, and consider using columns or putting a border or text box around each article to set it apart from the others.

If you want to dress up the newsletter you can add graphics, digital photos, borders, and different fonts (double-check that they are readable and will copy well). Be sure to select graphics that are age appropriate—that is, they can be "cuter" for parents of young children but should be more sophisticated for parents of high school students.

The format should be attractive with a balanced, uncluttered layout. Take the time to sketch out several different layout options and choose the one you like best. Once you have a suitable format and have published your first newsletter you can reuse the same pattern each month by simply cutting and pasting your new articles and headlines.

One last word about length—one page is sufficient for a newsletter, though some teachers choose to write longer tomes. A one-page format almost guarantees that parents will read it and that you will be able to come up with enough appealing articles to fill each issue.

Additional Suggestions

Class newsletters do not have to be weekly or even biweekly. They can be published once a month or even once or twice per grading period or semester.

Copying the newsletter in black and white is just fine, but color copies or copying on colored paper will certainly enhance its appearance.

You can send the newsletters home with your students or surface mail them to each family. You can also ask parents if they would prefer receiving the newsletter by e-mail, though in light of the spam blitz that most computer users face on a daily basis, it may be a risky option because some nonspam e-mails can be accidentally overlooked and discarded before reading, and sometimes attachments don't open properly on different operating systems.

An additional tip is to keep a Newsletter Idea Notebook where each month you can make notes of article ideas and store items of interest to include in the upcoming newsletter. Jot down any ideas as you think of them, and by the end of the month you'll most likely have lots of viable options from which to choose.

Of course, a class newsletter written in English, like any other print material you use to communicate with parents, is not useful to parents from non-English-speaking households, so if you are able to have the newsletter translated, so much the better.

One final word about confidentiality: If you plan to use photos of students in the newsletter and your school does not ask parents to sign a blanket photo release form at the beginning of the school year, you may want to send parents a letter requesting permission to use photos and names of students. Or you can inform them of this plan in your introductory letter by stating, "I plan to create and send home a monthly class newsletter chock full of important and interesting information. I may include photos of your child and articles about positive accomplishments, activities, and good news in which your child's name may appear, so if this is not acceptable to you, please let me know. I hope you will enjoy reading about our exciting school year!" Be sure to check with your administrator if you have any uncertainty about which permission route to take.

Class Newsletter Review Checklist

- ☐ Collect ideas for articles during each month in your Newsletter Idea Notebook.
- ☐ Select five to six varied ideas and write an article for each idea.
- ☐ Design a simple but attractive format for your newsletter using Microsoft Word or another newsletter template.
- ☐ Insert identifying information—title, your name, class, school, school address and phone number, your e-mail address, the date, and your signature graphic.
- ☐ Arrange the articles in a balanced layout.
- ☐ Add additional graphics or photos if desired.
- ☐ Paste new articles into your class newsletter format for each new issue.

Sample Materials

In Figure 4.5, Ms. Kamerling has included a variety of articles targeting the interests of the parents of her prekindergarten students. She teaches a class that is half students with special needs and half typically developing students, so she's chosen articles that would be of interest to all of the parents. Her newsletter is simple yet attractively designed using Microsoft Word and uses a table to frame the articles. Ms. Kamerling usually copies the newsletter on colored paper.

In Figure 4.6, Ms. Kreitz's second grade class newsletter features articles on current and future activities. In Figure 4.7, Ms. Williamson uses Microsoft PowerPoint to create her class newsletter. This two-page newsletter explains the Peer Buddies program, introduces her new classroom management system, and tells parents about the importance of having hygiene routines for her intermediate level students.

Ms. Fraley's Class Newsletter (Figure 4.8) has a balanced and attractive layout and includes a "Quote of the Month." Mrs. Gossett's single-page middle school class newsletter (Figure 4.9) packs in a lot of articles about such school subjects as science, nutrition, and language arts. She used Microsoft Word and added text boxes and graphics to create an attractive layout.

Ms. Gavarkavich's class newsletter (Figure 4.10) also presents a variety of interesting articles, including an introduction to a new staff member.

Figure 4.5 Class Newsletter—Prekindergarten

Ms. Kamerling's PreK Class News

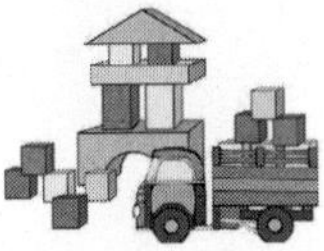

Cindy Kamerling
School
Address/Phone/E-mail
April 8, 2006

We Charted the Weather

Every day in March we observed the weather, chose the correct symbol, and put it on a pictograph. We found out which types of weather were more or less frequent, and we talked about dressing appropriately and predicting weather based on the results of our observations. This unit combined science, math, and daily living skills.

Mrs. Jones, Speech Therapist

Did you know that Mrs. Jones comes to our class twice a week to work with us on conversation skills? The students select a topic, such as pets or favorite foods, and each student takes a turn at asking and answering questions and making related comments. We work on making eye contact while talking and listening carefully. We've had some very lively discussions!

A Good Web Page: Social Skills

Parents of preschoolers are often concerned about teaching their children to show nice manners when visiting friends and at family gatherings.

The Web site www.kidsmanners.com offers many good suggestions for practicing good social skills with your child. There's even a checklist with pictures of social skills for many occasions.

A Simple Snack Your Child Can Prepare at Home

Kids love to prepare food, and letting them practice this skill at home helps with their independence. A piece of bread, raisins, peanut butter or jam, carrot strips, a few cheese cubes, and a blunt dip spreader are all your child will need to create an open-faced sandwich with an actual face on it. It's both healthful and fun to make and eat!

Question of the Month:

My child refuses to wear a hat in the cold weather—What should I do? One suggestion is to give your child a choice of hats each day. Make a game of it, and let him or her put the unchosen hats on a stuffed animal or doll. When purchasing hats, make sure they fit comfortably and that the material is not scratchy or irritating. Praise your child for putting on the hat and keeping it on.

Switch-Operated Toys in Our Classroom

Ten of our toys have been adapted with switches so that our students with motor challenges can operate them easily and play independently and with other students during free time. If you have any toys at home that have sound, visuals, or movement that you'd like to donate to us, we can have them adapted. Thanks!

Figure 4.6   Class Newsletter—Elementary School Learning Disabilities

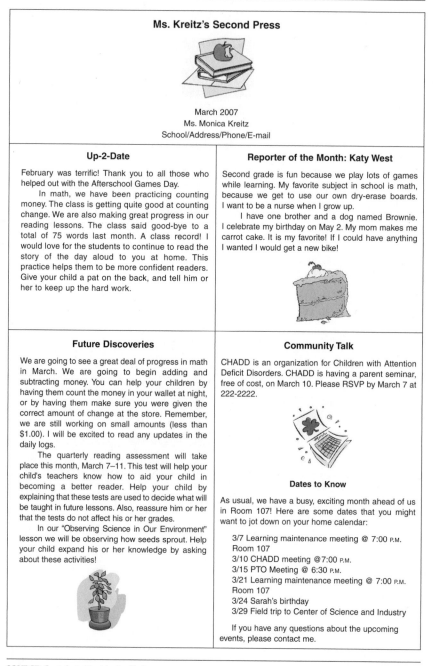

Ms. Kreitz's Second Press

March 2007
Ms. Monica Kreitz
School/Address/Phone/E-mail

Up-2-Date

February was terrific! Thank you to all those who helped out with the Afterschool Games Day.

In math, we have been practicing counting money. The class is getting quite good at counting change. We are also making great progress in our reading lessons. The class said good-bye to a total of 75 words last month. A class record! I would love for the students to continue to read the story of the day aloud to you at home. This practice helps them to be more confident readers. Give your child a pat on the back, and tell him or her to keep up the hard work.

Reporter of the Month: Katy West

Second grade is fun because we play lots of games while learning. My favorite subject in school is math, because we get to use our own dry-erase boards. I want to be a nurse when I grow up.

I have one brother and a dog named Brownie. I celebrate my birthday on May 2. My mom makes me carrot cake. It is my favorite! If I could have anything I wanted I would get a new bike!

Future Discoveries

We are going to see a great deal of progress in math in March. We are going to begin adding and subtracting money. You can help your children by having them count the money in your wallet at night, or by having them make sure you were given the correct amount of change at the store. Remember, we are still working on small amounts (less than $1.00). I will be excited to read any updates in the daily logs.

The quarterly reading assessment will take place this month, March 7–11. This test will help your child's teachers know how to aid your child in becoming a better reader. Help your child by explaining that these tests are used to decide what will be taught in future lessons. Also, reassure him or her that the tests do not affect his or her grades.

In our "Observing Science in Our Environment" lesson we will be observing how seeds sprout. Help your child expand his or her knowledge by asking about these activities!

Community Talk

CHADD is an organization for Children with Attention Deficit Disorders. CHADD is having a parent seminar, free of cost, on March 10. Please RSVP by March 7 at 222-2222.

Dates to Know

As usual, we have a busy, exciting month ahead of us in Room 107! Here are some dates that you might want to jot down on your home calendar:

3/7 Learning maintenance meeting @ 7:00 P.M. Room 107
3/10 CHADD meeting @7:00 P.M.
3/15 PTO Meeting @ 6:30 P.M.
3/21 Learning maintenance meeting @ 7:00 P.M. Room 107
3/24 Sarah's birthday
3/29 Field trip to Center of Science and Industry

If you have any questions about the upcoming events, please contact me.

SOURCE: Contributed by Monica Kreitz.

Figure 4.7 Class Newsletter—Elementary School Special Needs

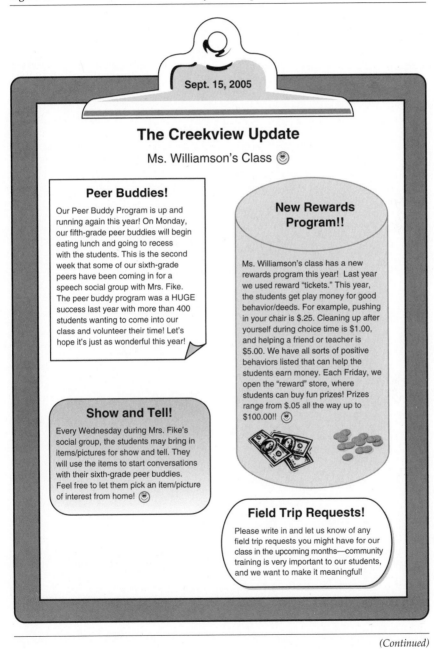

Sept. 15, 2005

The Creekview Update

Ms. Williamson's Class

Peer Buddies!

Our Peer Buddy Program is up and running again this year! On Monday, our fifth-grade peer buddies will begin eating lunch and going to recess with the students. This is the second week that some of our sixth-grade peers have been coming in for a speech social group with Mrs. Fike. The peer buddy program was a HUGE success last year with more than 400 students wanting to come into our class and volunteer their time! Let's hope it's just as wonderful this year!

Show and Tell!

Every Wednesday during Mrs. Fike's social group, the students may bring in items/pictures for show and tell. They will use the items to start conversations with their sixth-grade peer buddies. Feel free to let them pick an item/picture of interest from home!

New Rewards Program!!

Ms. Williamson's class has a new rewards program this year! Last year we used reward "tickets." This year, the students get play money for good behavior/deeds. For example, pushing in your chair is $.25. Cleaning up after yourself during choice time is $1.00, and helping a friend or teacher is $5.00. We have all sorts of positive behaviors listed that can help the students earn money. Each Friday, we open the "reward" store, where students can buy fun prizes! Prizes range from $.05 all the way up to $100.00!!

Field Trip Requests!

Please write in and let us know of any field trip requests you might have for our class in the upcoming months—community training is very important to our students, and we want to make it meaningful!

(Continued)

Figure 4.7 (Continued)

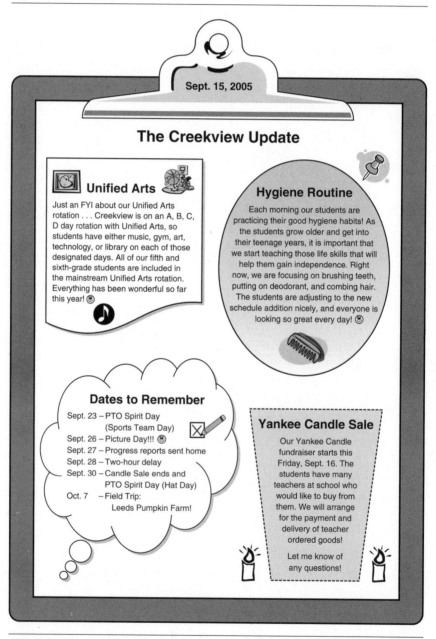

SOURCE: Contributed by Lindsay Williamson.

Figure 4.8   Class Newsletter—Elementary School Severe Disabilities

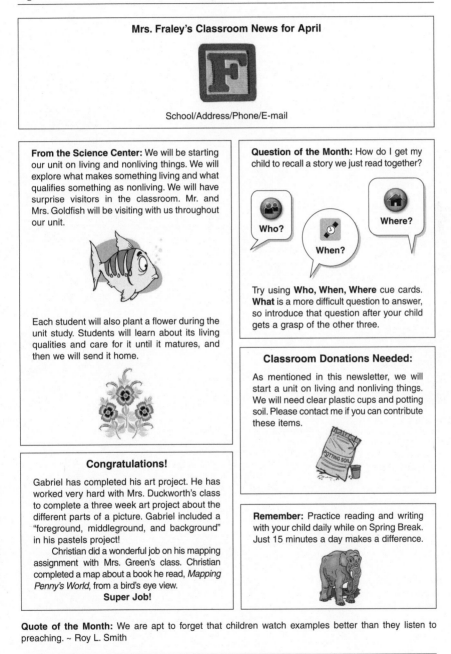

Mrs. Fraley's Classroom News for April

School/Address/Phone/E-mail

From the Science Center: We will be starting our unit on living and nonliving things. We will explore what makes something living and what qualifies something as nonliving. We will have surprise visitors in the classroom. Mr. and Mrs. Goldfish will be visiting with us throughout our unit.

Each student will also plant a flower during the unit study. Students will learn about its living qualities and care for it until it matures, and then we will send it home.

Congratulations!

Gabriel has completed his art project. He has worked very hard with Mrs. Duckworth's class to complete a three week art project about the different parts of a picture. Gabriel included a "foreground, middleground, and background" in his pastels project!

Christian did a wonderful job on his mapping assignment with Mrs. Green's class. Christian completed a map about a book he read, *Mapping Penny's World*, from a bird's eye view.
Super Job!

Question of the Month: How do I get my child to recall a story we just read together?

Who?   **When?**   **Where?**

Try using **Who, When, Where** cue cards. **What** is a more difficult question to answer, so introduce that question after your child gets a grasp of the other three.

Classroom Donations Needed:

As mentioned in this newsletter, we will start a unit on living and nonliving things. We will need clear plastic cups and potting soil. Please contact me if you can contribute these items.

Remember: Practice reading and writing with your child daily while on Spring Break. Just 15 minutes a day makes a difference.

Quote of the Month: We are apt to forget that children watch examples better than they listen to preaching. ~ Roy L. Smith

SOURCE: Contributed by Goldie Fraley.

Figure 4.9 Class Newsletter—Middle School Intellectual Disabilities

Mrs. Gretchen Gossett's Class Newsletter
February 2006

Jacob Knocks 'Em Down

Congratulations to Jacob Smith for contributing to the seventh-grade bowling team's victory over Snow Middle School in the seventh-grade tournament.

Jacob bowled one game of 185 and another of 190 to lead his team with most points in the tournament.

Healthy Bodies Healthy Minds

We will be starting an intensive health and nutrition unit at the end of November. During this unit we will be discussing, among other things, healthy alternatives to many of the popular junk food snacks that are marketed toward our children.

Parent volunteer opportunities are available to donate snack materials, prepare snacks to send to school, or come to class and lead a "snack-making workshop." Please contact me by phone or e-mail if you are able to volunteer in any capacity.

Introducing: Write Your Own Quiz!

Seventh graders should be aware of the world around them, and we would like to encourage parents and their seventh-grade children to watch the news and/or read the newspaper (paper or online). Each Tuesday students will write a summary about a particular current event and share that summary during a class discussion.

The students' summaries will then be compiled into a weekly current events quiz for our social studies class.

This way we will know what is going on in the world around us—and we will know what our seventh graders view as important.

Write Your Own Quiz begins on March 1, so let's get current!

Science News

Science classes are working on many hands-on labs. The students completed the ice cube experiments, in which they had to determine which of two liquids of choice would melt an ice cube faster at room temperature.

They will be working with the periodic table of chemical symbols and the history of the table, as well as mass, volume, and density.

All classes have begun planning projects for this year's science fair, which will take place on the evening of December 16, 2006. More information on the fair will be handed out in science classes.

Class Book Club Started by Students

Mandy Charles and Billy Ling have started a book club for our class. Each month the club will read a book recommended by our librarian.

Students wishing to participate will read the book and meet in my classroom during one of their study halls to discuss their reactions to the book.

Language arts extra credit will be awarded to all students who actively participate.

The book for February is The Doll People by Ann Martin.

Mrs. Gretchen Gossett
School
Address
Phone and e-mail

SOURCE: Contributed by Gretchen Gossett.

Figure 4.10 Class Newsletter—Middle School Special Needs

Seventh Grade—Ms. Gavarkavich's
Room 8 April Newsletter

April 1, 2007
School
Address
Phone and e-mail

Meet Mrs. Ridenour

This month, we have acquired a new staff member, Mrs. Ridenour. She is a speech therapist who will be working directly with our class once a week. Mrs. Ridenour is a graduate of the Ohio State University and is very excited to be working with us. She has extensive training and is very good at what she does. With her help, we hope to increase language skills in our classroom and develop better conversation skills. If your child needs one-on-one speech work, she will be available to begin sessions right away.

Trip to the Theater

To go along with our unit on plays, we will be taking a class trip to the theater to see *Grease* during the last week of this month. This will be a very exciting opportunity for our class, as they will get to see one of the plays we have been working on put into action. I have also set up a session for our students to meet the cast after we view the play. Any parents who would like to accompany us as chaperones would be welcome. I will be sending a letter home with more details and a tear off form for anyone interested.

And the Winner is . . .

As many of you know, an artwork competition was held throughout our school district. The competition asked students to create a work of art that they felt best represented them. They were able to use any materials they wished. I would like to proudly announce the winner of that competition, Tucker Daniels. Tucker is a member of our class, and it was great to see one of our students win this competition. He constructed a clay model of himself fishing, which is one of his favorite activities. The model will be on display in our classroom for the next couple of weeks.

Swim for Diabetes

Coming up in our community is the yearly Swim for Diabetes. This event will be held at the YMCA on Fifth Ave. on April 27. I participate in this program every year, and I would like to welcome any of our students or their family members to join me in this great cause. There is no fee to participate, and if you wish you may find sponsors to help you raise money. This is a very relaxed activity, and everyone is welcome to participate. I know that our students would be very proud of helping out others in the community in this way. Please contact me if you are interested.

(Continued)

Figure 4.10 (Continued)

Web Page of the Month

While doing some research recently, I came upon a great Web site that I feel would benefit many of our families. The Web site is titled "Interactive Games," and the address is http://www.multiplication.com. Since we have been working on multiplication this would be a great supplemental Web site for students to use at home. There are many areas and games that students can participate in that would help to build their multiplication skills. These interactive games are quite entertaining, so students will not even feel like they are doing schoolwork.

Classroom News

I am starting my master's degree program. As part of my program, I will be doing some extra social studies enrichment activities during the school day as part of my graduate assignments. I will be collecting some data, but no student names will be recorded and all individual results will be kept confidential. I appreciate the help I am receiving from my students in attaining this goal, and I know they will benefit from these special activities that I have designed for them.

SOURCE: Contributed by Krista Gavarkavich.

Personalized Written Communication and Interaction

- Weekly Progress Report (Strategy 8)
- Parent Appreciation Letter (Strategy 9)
- Print Resource Letter (Strategy 10)
- Internet Resource Letter (Strategy 11)
- E-mail Communication (Strategy 12)

STRATEGY 8: WEEKLY PROGRESS REPORT

Keeping parents informed of their child's educational progress is a good idea for several reasons. First and foremost, parents are interested in their children's progress and appreciate it when the teacher keeps them updated. Second, a regular progress report can signal parents when their child is experiencing difficulties or falling behind *before* the problem increases or reaches crisis proportions. The advance notice afforded by a progress report shows parents that you consider them important partners in monitoring their child's progress and allows them to provide additional help for their child when necessary.

Send the Report Weekly

Why not use a daily, rather than weekly, reporting form? Some teachers actually do send a note home to each parent every day, and that certainly is commendable. But creating a daily message for each student can be an unreasonable demand of time and paperwork, given the teacher's already heavy workload. Also, tracking most students' skills and behaviors on a weekly basis can be just as valid and useful, barring an unusual incident or instance of regression.

Use a Structured Format

So how do you provide a weekly update to parents that does not require a huge amount of time to prepare, yet still gives parents a good overview of their child's performance and progress? The answer is to use a format that has structure. While some teachers write a freeform account, I think a structured individual weekly progress report is a better communication vehicle because it is faster to fill out, easier to read, and more sustainable over time than creating extensive narrative accounts—a practice so time-consuming that its use is often discontinued after the first month or two. Another benefit of using a structured format is that it can be comprehensive, and in this way it also cues you to address and assess all areas of the student's educational program and services each week.

It's not difficult to design a clear and simple one-page individual weekly progress report. A grid or checklist format with a clear rating code or system gives parents a quick overview of their child's progress organized by curricular area, behavior, and/or task (e.g., reading, language arts, math, motor skills, science, daily living skills, social skills, communication, homework completion, or orientation and mobility) whether the student is served in a self-contained class, a resource room, an inclusive setting, or at a vocational field site. A space for comments allows the teacher and parents to exchange additional qualitative information on an as-needed basis.

Weekly Progress Report Review Checklist

☐ Determine the key academic/subject/functional skill areas for weekly tracking.
☐ Set up a table or grid covering 5 days with 6–10 skills/subject areas.
☐ Determine a rating or coding system to indicate levels of performance.
☐ Add header and footer information for names, dates, and comments from both teacher(s) and parent.

Sample Materials

The eleven samples included in this section are geared to four different grade levels and reflect different disability categories and service delivery options. Several reports have been filled out collaboratively by the special and regular class teachers; some are blank and some have been filled in with data. One sample highlights some changes in modifications and adaptations in the student's program that the parent is alerted to.

Unlike most of the other examples that follow, the prekindergarten report (Figure 5.1) is set up as an overall weekly report without specific daily evaluations. Mrs. Fried feels that this more general approach is appropriate at the preschool level.

Ms. Reid's elementary example (Figure 5.2) targets four main academic areas as well as cooperation, social behavior, and promptness. Ms. Kreitz's report (Figure 5.3) adds two more areas—art and health—for her weekly reports but uses a slightly more open-ended format. Mrs. Bourke's middle school report (Figure 5.4) is specifically designed for her student Brett, who has learning disabilities and is focusing on

Figure 5.1   Weekly Progress Report—Prekindergarten

Mrs. S. Fried
School
Address
Phone and e-mail

Student   Lucy Berger

Week of   May 10–14

	Excellent Participation	Very Good Effort	Showing Improvement	Needs to Work on This Area	Comments
Morning circle time	X				Super job!
Pre-academic activities		X			Loves writing
Free choice activity time				X	Needs to work on sustained attention
Fine motor activities	X				
Large motor activities— Indoor and outdoor		X			
Art and music activities		X			
Communication skills			X		Using more words and signs appropriately
Interactions with adults		X			
Social interactions with peers			X		Starting to initiate more play

Teacher comments:

Lucy is doing very well overall and continues to show significant improvement in communication and social interaction with her peers. Lucy continues to work on choosing an independent activity during free time and sticking with it for the 10-minute period. Perhaps you could encourage some brief periods of free play at home too.

P.S. The book about orangutans that Lucy brought in to share was perfect—the kids loved the story. Thank you!

Parent comments: _____

organizational and self-management skills. In Figure 5.5, Ms. Leek uses a format that reflects the more functional educational needs of students with severe and multiple disabilities. Ms. Leek chooses to use this report on a daily rather than weekly basis. Figure 5.6 also demonstrates a weekly report tailored to a student learning a more functional curriculum, while Ms. Williamson's form (Figure 5.7) is used with students with mild intellectual disabilities.

Ms. Peterson, the high school resource room teacher of Marsha, a student with learning disabilities who is included for all of her subject areas, collaborated with the regular class teachers to come up with an easy-to-use report (Figure 5.8). Each teacher e-mails his or her weekly results to Ms. Peterson each Friday so she can enter all the data and add some overall comments.

The final three weekly progress reports (Figures 5.9, 5.10, and 5.11) are used at the high school level and are targeted for use with students with mild, moderate, and severe cognitive disabilities respectively.

STRATEGY 9: PARENT APPRECIATION LETTER

Once in a while a student sends me a thank-you note. Sometimes these notes are handwritten—nowadays more likely to be e-mailed—but they're always a very pleasant surprise and much appreciated no matter what the mode of transmission. Honestly, these letters make my day—a little positive reinforcement goes a long way!

A student might thank me for doing a small thing, such as writing a reference letter or taking the time to listen to his problem or a challenge with which he is dealing. Or a student may tell me she really enjoyed a class I taught or thank me for helping her with something more substantial, such as helping her obtain a summer job or teaching position or providing assistance with another significant matter over the course of their college experience.

I keep these notes in a file in my office, and periodically, especially when I've had a trying day, I take it out and read through these thoughtful messages. I put a lot of effort into being a good teacher—it's a very demanding job if you do it right—and it feels good when my efforts are recognized in this way.

Like teaching, parenting can be a challenging and exhausting enterprise, especially for those with a child whose special needs require more intensive and diversified parental efforts over a longer period of time than when parenting typically developing offspring.

In addition, many parents of children with disabilities have a history of receiving negative or problem-oriented letters and phone calls from school concerning their child. It's probably a rare occasion to receive positive feedback or some type of "good news" from the school. These parents can't help but feel, most often without basis, that their children's difficulties are a poor reflection on them and an indictment of their parenting skills. This type of perceived feedback makes their jobs as parents even more stressful.

What can you, the teacher, do to recognize and show appreciation for the efforts, endurance, and successes of parents of children with special needs? A parent appreciation letter that celebrates their child's achievement, whether big or small, is a wonderful way to tell parents that you share in their joy when their child takes a step forward and to congratulate them on their contribution to this happy event.

Figure 5.2 Weekly Progress Report—Elementary School Learning Disabilities/Emotional or Behavioral Disorders

Ms. Lindsay Reid
School
Address
Phone and e-mail

Student _____   Date _____

Teacher _____

	Monday	Tuesday	Wednesday	Thursday	Friday
Cooperation within a group					
Behavior during class					
Academic efforts	Math: Reading:	Math: Reading:	Math: Reading:	Math: Reading:	Math: Reading:
	Science: Social Studies:	Science: Social Studies:	Science: Social Studies:	Science: Social Studies:	Science: Social Studies:
Promptness to class					
Teacher comments					
Parent/ Guardian comments					

5 = Excellent   Teacher signature _____

4 = Good   Parent/Guardian signature _____

3 = Satisfactory

2 = Poor

1 = Unacceptable

SOURCE: Contributed by Lindsay Reid.

Figure 5.3   Weekly Progress Report—Elementary School

Ms. Monica Kreitz
School
Address
Phone and e-mail

Week of _____

Dear Parent(s) and/or Guardian(s) of _____,

Hello! As you know we have had a busy week of learning, but now it is time for the week's stats!

The **Reading** Center: _____

The **Math** Lab: _____

The **Writing** Studio: _____

The **Science** Lab: _____

The **Health** Beat: _____

In the World of **Social Studies**: _____

The **Art** Studio: _____

Other: _____

An area your child did well in this week was

_____

_____

Your child could use some assistance with

_____

_____

Please contact me by phone or e-mail with any questions, delights, or concerns!

Happy weekend,

Ms. Kreitz

SOURCE: Contributed by Monica Kreitz.

Figure 5.4   Weekly Progress Report: Organizational Skills—Middle School Learning Disabilities

Mrs. Bourke
School
Address
Phone and e-mail

For Student <u>Brett Hartley</u>   **Week of** <u>October 10–15</u>

During class changes (3 random checks per day for #1–5)	Monday Y = YES N = NO	Tuesday	Wednesday	Thursday	Friday
1. Two sharp pencils and pen in case	NNN	YNY	YYN	YYY	YYY
2. All work papers in correct ring binder sections	NNY	YNN	YYN	YYY	YYY
3. Homework assignments in folder	YNN	NNN	YYY	YYN	YYY
4. Backpack packed and fully zipped	YYY	NYN	YNY	YNY	NYY
5. On time for classes	YNN	YNN	NYY	YYY	YYY
6. On time for bus	Y	N	Y	Y	Y
7. Took home coat, backpack, and clarinet	Y	Y	Y	Y	Y
Total % YES	47%	35%	76%	88%	94%

Teacher comments: After our phone conversation on Tuesday evening and your talk with Brett about the importance of organization and punctuality, he showed great improvement for the rest of the week. I'm letting Brett use my computer to record his progress at the end of the day, and he seems very pleased with his chart results. Thanks for your cooperation and support.

Mrs. Bourke

Parent comments:

_____

_____

_____

Figure 5.5   Daily Progress Report—Middle School Severe Disabilities

Ms. Amy Leek
School
Address
Phone and e-mail

Dear Parents,

This individual daily progress report comprises spaces for comments about each area of your child's education. Feel free to read my comments and reply in the space provided. I will send this report to you each day to keep you updated on your child's progress.

Your student _____

	Day/Date:
IEP goals and objectives	
Classroom behavior	
Functional academics	
Specials	
Homework	
Meal time	
Misc.	
Teacher comments	
Parent comments	

SOURCE: Contributed by Amy Leek.

Figure 5.6   Weekly Progress Report—Middle School Severe Disabilities

Mrs. Vickie Calland
School
Address
Phone and e-mail

Student _____   Date _____

Task	Monday	Tuesday	Wednesday	Thursday	Friday
Writes personal information					
Performs hygiene tasks					
Follows verbal directions					
Stays on task—Classroom					
Stays on task—Worksite					
Makes acceptable comments					
Maintains appropriate space					
Maintains appropriate speaking volume					

Rating System: B = Below target level, T = Target level, H = High achievement level

Parent comments:
Signature: Date:

SOURCE: Contributed by Vickie Calland.

Figure 5.7 Weekly Progress Report—Middle School Learning Disabilities/Intellectual Disabilities

Ms. Lindsay Williamson
School
Address
Phone and e-mail

Student _____   **Date** _____

Task	Monday	Tuesday	Wednesday	Thursday	Friday
Classroom behavior					
Effort and cooperation					
Punctuality					
Academic performance	Math_____ Lang Arts____ Science_____ Soc Stud____ Voc_____	Math_____ Lang Arts____ Science_____ Soc Stud____ Voc_____	Math_____ Lang Arts____ Science_____ Soc Stud____ Voc_____	Math_____ Lang Arts____ Science_____ Soc Stud____ Voc_____	Math_____ Lang Arts____ Science_____ Soc Stud____ Voc_____
Task and homework completion					
Overall					

5 = Excellent   2 = Needs Improvement

4 = Good   1 = Unsatisfactory

3 = Average   NA = Not Applicable

Teacher comments:

Parent comments:

Parent signature: _____

SOURCE: Contributed by Lindsay Williamson.

Figure 5.8   Weekly Progress Report—Middle School Intellectual Disabilities

Ms. Jane Peterson
School
Address
Phone and e-mail
For: <u>Marsha Mayes</u>

Week of _____ February 3 _____

Class	Participation	Homework	Test/Quiz	Comments	Teacher's Initials
Biology	1	1	Test = 67%		RLS
English	2	3	Quiz = A	Great job!	LDH
Speech	2	2	NA	Late to class once this week	FT
American History	2	2	NA	On target	IHJ
Algebra	3	3	Quiz = 82%	Keeps showing improvement	PST
P.E.	1	NA	NA	Refused to change for class on MW	TAC
Music	2	Listening Log not turned in	NA		MN

3 = Outstanding, 2 = Acceptable, 1 = Below target goal

Comments from the Resource Room: Marsha is doing quite well in most areas but needs more work in biology. Please encourage her to bring the textbook and all of her notes to the Resource Room so we can review. Also, please speak to Marsha about the situation in P. E. so we can get her on track there.

Ms. Jane Peterson

Parent comments:

_____

_____

_____

Figure 5.9   Weekly Progress Report—High School Learning Disabilities/Intellectual Disabilities

Ms. Jennifer Vaughn
School
Address
Phone and e-mail

Student Susie Jones
Dates February 12–16, 2007
Intervention Specialist Jennifer Vaughn

5 = Excellent, 4 = Good, 3 = Acceptable, 2 = Needs improvement, 1 = Unacceptable
A = Student absent, - = No class

Subject	M	T	W	Th	F	Comments	Teacher Initials
Reading	5	5	5	5	4	Strong progress	B. R
Social studies	5	3	2	5	5		B. R.
Math	4	2	2	1	4	Needs to complete homework daily	B. D.
P.E.	5	–	–	–	–	Way to go!	L. L.
Music	–	5	–	–	–		S. P.
Art	2	–	–	–	–		E. S.
Lunch/Recess	2	3	5	4	4	Improvement shown in social skills	F. Y.

Additional comments from teachers:

_____

_____

_____

Parent comments:

_____

_____

_____

_____

SOURCE: Contributed by Jennifer Vaughn.

Figure 5.10 Weekly Progress Report—High School Severe Disabilities

Ms. April Walsh
School
Address
Phone and e-mail

Student's name _____   **Week of** _____

The following chart shows your student's weekly progress. I am using the following recording system:

+	=	Student did a great job!
–	=	Student needs improvement in this area.
NC	=	Student was noncompliant.
(blank)	=	We did not work on this area today.

	Monday	Tuesday	Wednesday	Thursday	Friday
Academic goals					
Cooperative play					
Personal hygiene					
Speech/Communication					
Community goals					
Walking group/Exercise					
Occupational therapy goals					
Physical therapy goals					
Other					

Comments/Needs/Special Requests

Parent:

Teacher:

SOURCE: Contributed by April Walsh.

Figure 5.11 Weekly Progress Report—High School Severe Disabilities

Ms. Megan Aikey
School
Address
Phone and e-mail

Student _____   Week of _____

Skill	Mon.	Tues.	Wed.	Thurs.	Fri.	Comments	Parent Comments
Time/Schedule							
Money/Banking							
Behavior at jobsite (A.M./P.M.)							
Behavior in class							
Grooming/Attire							
Lunch etiquette							
In-class job completion							

O = Outstanding

A = Acceptable

B = Below Target Goal

Additional comments/Concerns:

SOURCE: Contributed by Megan Aikey.

Make a Special Accomplishments Chart

An easy way to collect ideas for these letters is to use a chart, kept on a clipboard or in a notebook in a handy place in your classroom, to briefly record special student accomplishments that you notice on a daily basis. Then, each week or two, you can select one or more students whose parents will receive a parent appreciation letter from you.

A sample Special Accomplishments Chart, such as the following figure, filled in with examples from a range of grade levels, will help you make note of these special moments as they happen:

Student	Accomplishment and Significance	Date	Letter Sent to Parents?
Laura: preschool	Put her coat on without help and quickly while in her wheelchair before recess; this may seem like a small thing but it's a big step toward her achieving independence and fitting in with her peers.	10/6	Yes, 10/6
Martha: second grade	Inserted and kept her hearing aid in and turned on to proper volume every day without reminders; this is so important to her ability to comprehend instructions and lesson content; she was on top of everything this week.	10/6	Yes, 10/6
Akeelah: fourth grade	Spelling test improvement—earned 100% on advanced grade level tests three weeks in a row in a subject she had been struggling with; she showed motivation and commitment to study every day at school and at home—her regular class teacher noted this progress.	10/6	Not yet
Carlos: seventh grade	Orientation and mobility—using his cane, Carlos successfully traveled from resource room to inclusion class on a different floor of the school building by himself; I know he's working on independent travel at home and out in the community; he expressed pride in his accomplishment and has mentioned that he may not need a buddy to accompany him to the restroom and lunchroom anymore!	10/9	Not yet
Lee: eighth grade	Social behavior—on several occasions, chose appropriate option (calmly moved on to the next section, came back later to work on difficult problem) when frustrated with written work, then tried again and was successful; politely asked teacher for help on another occasion; also helped a classmate make an appropriate choice; these behaviors will serve him well next year in high school.	10/15	Yes, 10/15
Branden: sophomore in high school	Vocational—at nursing home work-study placement, increased speed and accuracy of serving lunches to residents; served entire floor in a half-hour and still had time for some very nice conversations with the residents (they love and appreciate Branden and his nice sense of humor); got a rave review from his supervisor—possible future career?	10/16	Yes, 10/19
Jordan: senior in high school	Excelled in our math unit on handling checking and savings accounts; these skills will be so useful to her in the near future; she expressed an interest in having an actual bank account and learning more about budgeting.	10/16	Not yet

Parent Appreciation Letter Review Checklist

❐ Set up a Special Accomplishments Chart to record special achievements of your students on an ongoing basis.
❐ Select a student whose parents will be the recipient of an appreciation letter.
❐ Explain the purpose of letter.
❐ Identify the student's accomplishment.
❐ Explain why you are so pleased.
❐ Thank the parents for their help in this achievement.

Sample Materials

In the nine sample letters that follow, the accomplishments targeted for recognition include the following academic and social skills and range from prekindergarten through high school: self-dressing (Figure 5.12); inserting a hearing aid (Figure 5.13); helping others (Figure 5.14); preparation, planning, and assignment completion (Figures 5.15 and 5.16); dealing appropriately with frustration (Figure 5.17); initiating greetings (Figure 5.18); lacing shoes (Figure 5.19); and performance at a work-study placement (Figure 5.20).

Some of the letters (Figures 5.12, 5.13, 5.17, and 5.20) transform several of the accomplishments noted earlier in the Special Accomplishments Chart into complete parent appreciation letters. Note that all of the letters not only praise the students and their parents but also give a rationale for the importance of the achievement and provide a link between current activities and future success. Each letter uses a positive tone and conveys a spirit of teamwork between parents and teachers.

If you send a parent appreciation letter home by surface mail or with the student (rather than by e-mail), don't be surprised if your student tells you that your letter is now posted on her refrigerator for the entire family to enjoy.

Figure 5.12 Parent Appreciation Letter—Prekindergarten Orthopedic Impairments

Ms. Judy Shapiro
School
Address
Phone and e-mail

Dear Mr. and Mrs. Herman:

Today, just before the students were about to line up and go out for recess, I looked around to find Laura so I could help her put on her coat, hat, and mittens or ask one of her classmates to do so. I was very pleasantly surprised to find Laura already dressed, at the head of the line, and ready to go outside and play with her friends!

I asked Laura how she had accomplished this all so quickly, and she told me that she tried using the dressing method we had all been trying to teach her (but she had been resisting), and to her surprise she had gotten into her coat on the first try, and then was so excited she was able to quickly get the other items on and maneuver her wheelchair over to the line. She had a huge smile on her face, and so did I.

This small step toward Laura's independence is very significant because the satisfaction she experienced in doing this task by herself will motivate her to attempt other challenging tasks in the future. Her accomplishment has also allowed her to blend in appropriately and feel on the same par with her classmates as they ready themselves for our daily activities.

Thank you both for working with Laura on increasing her independence skills—our collaboration has really paid off.

I'm looking forward to seeing you at our upcoming conference next month.

Sincerely,

Judy Shapiro

Figure 5.13 Parent Appreciation Letter—Elementary School Hearing Impairments

Mrs. Stacy Walker
School
Address
Phone and e-mail

Dear Mr. Gonzales:

I just wanted to let you know that Martha has responded very well to our program that teaches her to insert her hearing aid and keep it in place and turned to the correct volume all day.

After several weeks of practice both at school and at home, Martha is now completely independent on this task and does not have to be reminded to do so. The checklist that Martha uses every morning and after lunch has allowed her to successfully monitor her own behavior, and I think this reminder should not even be necessary after she is successful for a few more weeks.

For the past few weeks, I have noticed that Martha responds to my instructions immediately, is following oral directions about her schoolwork correctly and well the first time they are given, and is interacting more with her classmates during small group work and during specials. To a great extent, her progress seems to have eliminated most of her confusion and frustration about what she needs to do while in class and what her classmates are saying to her that she previously misunderstood or missed entirely.

Please keep me informed after Martha's next visit to the audiologist so that I can make any necessary modifications to the use and care of her hearing aid.

Martha is a lovely girl who is a delight to have in my class. Thanks for all you've done to work with me on her "Aid-In" program.

Sincerely,

Mrs. Stacy Walker

Figure 5.14 Parent Appreciation Letter—Elementary School Intellectual Disabilities

Ms. Jennifer Vaughn
School
Address
Phone and e-mail

Dear Ms. Swift:

It is with much pleasure that I am writing to you concerning Billy's kindness to another student. Last week, one of Billy's fellow classmates dropped her pencil and crayon box on the floor just as we were getting ready for recess. All of the students were focused on lining up to get outside as quickly as possible. All of the students, that is, except for Billy.

Instead of walking past his classmate while she struggled to gather the many items she had dropped, Billy took the time to help her clean up the mess. He could have decided to ignore the student and get in line without any negative consequences, but instead he chose to help her. It is rare that an adult comes to the aid of a struggling citizen, much less a child who is anxious to get to the playground! I am impressed with Billy's initiative and consideration.

Finally, I want to commend you for instilling such compassion and kindness in your son. A caring disposition such as Billy demonstrated by helping another classmate is most certainly a reflection of the values you teach and model.

Sincerely,

Jennifer Vaughn

SOURCE: Contributed by Jennifer Vaughn.

Figure 5.15 Parent Appreciation Letter—Middle School Learning Disabilities

Ms. Melissa Konicki
School
Address
Phone and e-mail

Dear Mr. and Mrs. Goodman:

Parents often receive letters from school containing general information or perhaps acknowledgment of a concern. I feel that students who are making great strides do not always get the attention they deserve, so I'm writing you today to recognize and celebrate a positive achievement your child has accomplished.

I want to take this opportunity to let you know how much I appreciate Jonathan's effort in my class. He always comes to class prepared with the necessary materials as well as a positive attitude. He is not afraid to try new things and is supportive of his classmates' efforts to try as well. In addition, Jonathan has completed and turned in every assignment on time for the entire month!

Thank you for sharing your son with us. Jonathan is an asset to our classroom. He is a great role model for the other students and is a pleasure to be around. I thank you for your continued support and encouragement. You have much to be proud of!

Sincerely,

Melissa Konicki

SOURCE: Contributed by Melissa Konicki.

Figure 5.16   Parent Appreciation Letter—Middle School Learning Disabilities/Intellectual Disabilities

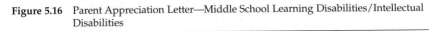

Ms. Sarah Miller
School
Address
Phone and e-mail

Dear Mr. Wade and Ms. Kingsbury:

I am writing this letter to inform you about the exciting progress that Ben has made over the past couple of weeks. As you know, one of Ben's goals on his IEP is to write assignments in his daily planner and complete in-class work and homework. In the past two weeks he has consistently added assignments to his planner without any reminders or prompts. Ben has also shown consistent effort with his in-class work. He has been trying to do the work independently first and if he is struggling will ask a teacher for assistance.

I am sure Ben has informed you each day that he receives a star on the star chart. For the past two weeks he has received a star every day, which has been very exciting for all of us. He received an award at the end of this week and last. That is a big improvement from earning an award only every three to four weeks.

Ben has come into school each day with all homework completed and materials ready to start the day. I have seen a positive change in his confidence and his overall mood, which has positively affected his interactions with his peers. I cannot tell you how proud I am of Benjamin. He has made a wonderful turnaround that is worthy of recognition. We have hung an Outstanding Worker award up in the classroom with his name and picture on it. It will remain there for the rest of the month.

I want to thank you for your continued support. Your help at home with his homework, continued encouragement, and consistency has really made a difference with Ben's academics. I am so very proud of Ben's success and accomplishments, and I can't wait to see what he will achieve next! Thanks again!

Best wishes,

Ms. Sarah Miller

SOURCE: Contributed by Sarah Miller.

Figure 5.17   Parent Appreciation Letter—Middle School Emotional or Behavioral
Disorders

Jeremy Baker
School
Address
Phone and e-mail

Dear Mr. and Dr. Darcy-Hubbard:

With senior high school fast approaching for Lee, we have all been concerned that some of his social behaviors would pose a problem for him in the coming years. To work on helping Lee deal with frustration in a more mature manner, I have been working with him to establish a problem-solving routine when he encounters work that is difficult or challenging for him to handle. I know that you have been following the same procedures with him at home so that he can easily utilize his adaptive strategies, no matter what the environment.

I am pleased to report to you that this week, on several occasions, Lee chose an appropriate option when he ran into difficult problems in doing his in-class biology work. As we had practiced, he tried the problem a second time and then calmly went on to solve the next problem in his packet. A few problems later he re-tackled the one he had skipped and this time was successful. On one occasion, he politely asked for my assistance and proceeded to work while waiting for me to come over to help him. His calm and appropriate handling of these problems made for a very pleasant class for him, for me, and for his classmates.

I also was so pleased to observe that when Lee noticed that the student sitting next to him was struggling with a problem, Lee spontaneously suggested that this student not get upset but keep working, return to the problem, and then ask the teacher if he needed help. Positive interactions of this kind will pave the way for Lee to develop a good social network in the high school setting.

Please tell Lee to keep up the good work, and thanks for your encouragement.

Sincerely,

Jeremy Baker

Figure 5.18 Parent Appreciation Letter—Middle School Severe Disabilities

Ms. Anna Bayert
School
Address
Phone and e-mail

Dear Mr. and Mrs. Smith:

I am writing to you because Sally has had a wonderful week, and I wanted to share her accomplishments with you. As you know, one of Sally's goals is to initiate at least one greeting a day at school. We have worked hard with Sally during the school year on this goal. At the beginning of the year, Sally needed constant reminders to greet her teachers and peers. Up until last week, we were using a visual prompt (holding up a reminder card) to encourage her to say "Hello."

This week has been a monumental week for Sally. She came in on Monday morning and said "Hello" without any prompts from us. She said this with a big smile on her face. We were so proud of her! She has begun to greet everyone now whenever she walks into a room. Sally went to art class this morning and greeted her classmates. This was the first time she had done so, and they were very excited. Many of them came over to her to give her high fives and other words of encouragement. Sally really enjoyed seeing her peers' reactions.

I know that you both have worked very hard on this goal with Sally, and I am just so pleased that she is on her way to mastering it. Every day this week Sally has come into our classroom with a big grin and a greeting. I am very impressed with her hard work and am excited that she is initiating interactions with her peers. Thank you for all of your hard work as well.

Best wishes,

Ms. Bayert

SOURCE: Contributed by Anna Bayert.

Figure 5.19   Parent Appreciation Letter—Elementary School Orthopedic Impairments

Ms. Christina Demetry
School
Address
Phone and e-mail

Dear Ms. Davis:

I am writing you with some exciting news. As you know, one of Olivia's IEP goals is for her to independently tie her own shoes. Today, we had a major breakthrough!

For the past few weeks we have been working with Olivia using a shoe tying prop. My staff and I created this prop by simply nailing a lace-up shoe onto a heavy board and coloring the strings red and black. By having the strings two different colors, we were able to verbally prompt Olivia through each step of the shoe tying process. For example, "Put the red shoelace over the black one." Every day Olivia showed improvement, needing fewer verbal prompts from my staff or me.

Well, today Olivia not only made it through each step without needing a single verbal prompt but also reached down and attempted to tie her own shoes, and she did it! I wish you could have heard the screams of joy coming from our classroom. The entire staff was on a high for the rest of the day. This accomplishment is just one more step that brings Olivia closer to having a happy and more independent life.

We want to thank you for your part in this major accomplishment. Without your continuous work with Olivia at home, we might not have reached this goal so quickly. Olivia's success in our classroom is truly a group effort.

Sincerely,

Christy Demetry

SOURCE: Contributed by Christina Demetry.

Figure 5.20 Parent Appreciation Letter—High School Severe Disabilities

Erin O'Malley
School
Address
Phone and e-mail

Dear Mr. and Mrs. Colby:

I got a phone call today from Branden's supervisor at the Crestview Nursing Home, where he has his twice-a-week work-study placement. Emily Craver was calling to tell me how pleased she was with Branden's performance during the past week.

First, Branden has increased the speed with which he serves lunch to the residents (an entire floor in less than half an hour!), and he delivers each meal to the correct individual each and every time.

Second, his appearance has been neat and professional, and he has complied perfectly with the rigorous hand-washing program Crestview has instituted.

Last, several of the residents have mentioned to Emily how much they enjoy Branden's outgoing personality and nice sense of humor. They look forward to Tuesdays and Thursdays when he delivers their meals and takes a few minutes to chat with them.

Branden's placement is going so well, and he seems to enjoy it immensely. He is such a people person, and I think he would be so successful in a job that involves interacting with and helping other people. He has mentioned to me that you both spend time discussing future vocational plans with him, and this kind of home support is so helpful in guiding our students into satisfying careers.

Please feel free to call me if you have any questions regarding this placement or the ones we're considering for next semester. Thanks for you help and support.

Sincerely,

Erin O'Malley

STRATEGY 10: PRINT RESOURCE LETTER

I recently spent an enlightening morning at our local Barnes and Noble bookstore. Sipping a coffee and armed with a tape measure, I stationed myself in the periodicals section and surveyed the entire 180 feet of 10-tiered magazine racks. End-to-end, all of these magazine racks would stretch more than half the length of a football field! The magazines were grouped in categories such as transportation, sports, science and nature, crafts, computers, women's interest, house/home, and the difficult-to-fathom heading "lifestyles." I had no idea there were so many magazines for animal lovers, hairstylists, bodybuilders, poets, and coin collectors. I was impressed and amazed to see the huge array of periodicals available to the public.

But what I was actually trying to determine was which magazines might have articles relating to children, parents, teaching, or people with disabilities. Over the course of several visits to the store, my eyes were drawn to a feature article in *Parent and Child* magazine that described a variety of creative ways to stimulate a young child's five senses during the summer months. This information, presented in a concise and catchy fashion, would surely be helpful to parents of children in preschool or the primary grades. An article in *Parenting* focused on "Raising a Compassionate Child," a subject that many parents of children, both typically developing and with disabilities, would find useful. *Parents* featured an article called "Juvenile Justice" that described a technique of providing natural consequences for misbehavior and using helpful correction procedures. Another *Parent and Child* issue had a great article on its picks for the best new toys, books, and videos, and *Newsweek* magazine featured autism in its cover story.

Like many educators, I love to read. I subscribe to our local newspaper and to several weekly and monthly magazines. I get eight or nine professional journals. One of my favorite resources is *Exceptional Parent* magazine, a timely, readable, and reliable monthly publication filled with articles for parents with a wide range of interests and needs. Recent issues of *Exceptional Parent* have had excellent articles on topics such as bullying, Klinefelter's syndrome, epilepsy, diet and nutrition, and financial planning. I also subscribe to several special education e-mail newsletters that identify and provide links to interesting articles from magazines, journals, and newspapers from all over the country.

In addition to regularly perusing these periodicals for materials that are potentially useful to parents, I am always looking for free print materials that would be useful to parents from other sources. I have found many great booklets, fact sheets, and newsletters at the pediatrician's office, at the public library, at K–12 schools where my students are doing field placements, at our regional resource center, at conferences and conventions, and even at the local art museum. I organize these materials in a file for easy access, adding new finds and tossing out materials that have become outdated. Some of the topics covered by these print materials include homework assistance; physical therapy; guardianship issues; academic content standards; helpful information on leaving a child with a babysitter; home science experiments; assistance with selecting communication devices; lifting, carrying, and positioning techniques; and functional math activities.

There are so many print resources available that can provide helpful information to parents, and teachers can connect parents with useful and timely articles, brochures, or other print materials that they come across. But you don't want to flood parents with information that may or may not be pertinent or of interest to them. So when you find a resource that you feel would be helpful to particular parents, send it to them along with a print resource letter that clearly identifies and briefly explains the publication and why you think it might be of interest to them. In this way, you will make the information more meaningful and immediately accessible to the parent.

Another idea is to create a print resource library in your classroom or another convenient place at your school where parents can go to copy or borrow items of interest. Be sure to seek and include materials in other languages for parents whose home language is not English.

Print Resource Letter Review Checklist

❏ Determine a parent's need for information in a particular area.
❏ Identify several relevant articles, brochures, or fact sheets.
❏ Evaluate the usefulness and credibility of the materials.
❏ Select the most appropriate print material for a particular parent.
❏ Write an introductory explanation for the parent.
❏ Describe the print material and its potential usefulness.
❏ Write a closing for the letter.
❏ Attach a copy of the print material to the letter.

Sample Materials

The six samples that follow (Figures 5.21–5.26) present a variety of topics found in print materials such as educational toy selection, sibling issues, special needs summer camps, self-determination, adaptive equipment, and independent living skills that teachers bring to the attention of a particular parent. Each teacher has made a clear connection between the child's and his or her family's needs and the content of the print material.

Figure 5.21   Print Resource Letter—Prekindergarten Autism

Kathy Lawrence
School
Address
Phone and e-mail

Dear Dr. Andros and Mr. Detonte:

As children's birthdays and holidays approach, parents often ask me for suggestions of toys that would be appropriate for toddlers and preschoolers with special needs.

As this topic came up last week when you dropped off Ginger at school, I'm attaching several recent articles from *Exceptional Parent* (*EP*) magazine that not only describe a variety of interesting and engaging toys but also explain when and why they are good choices and how they can be used.

For example, in the article "Toys to Support Children With Autism" that I've attached, the author describes several toys that facilitate verbalization and independent play, two areas that Ginger is working on at school and at home. I've also included the Annual Toy Issue of *Exceptional Parent* that features several articles focusing on the use of puppets, building blocks, and other toys as wonderful teaching tools in these two areas. I'll keep looking for other articles for you on this topic in upcoming *EP*s and other reliable sources.

Please keep the "Toys to Support Children With Autism" article, but I'd appreciate it if you would return the *EP* toy issue in a few weeks when you are finished with it. Be sure to let me know if you have any questions about these materials, and give Ginger a big birthday hug from me.

Sincerely,

Kathy Lawrence

Figure 5.22   Print Resource Letter—Elementary School Intellectual Disabilities

Mr. J. Riley
School
Address
Phone and e-mail

Dear Mrs. Jefferson:

As I was reading this month's issue of *Exceptional Parent,* I noticed an article that made me think of you and your family. It's called "Lessons from My Brother" by Valencia Clay, the sister of Carlton, who has Down syndrome.

The article is a very inspiring account of the positive way that Carlton's mother nurtured and set high expectations for her son and how much her daughter Valencia learned from observing their inter-actions. Now Valencia is a doctor and reflects on how much she learned from her mom and brother's relationship and how she can apply what she learned to her practice of medicine.

Of course, I thought of you not only because of what a wonderful mom you are to Devin but also because you mentioned to me that your daughter Destiny has expressed a desire to choose a medical career. I think she'd be very interested in reading this article also.

Devin has had another great week at school, and we're all looking forward to seeing you next Thursday when you come to help out with our hands-on science project.

Sincerely,

Jeff Riley

Figure 5.23 Print Resource Letter—Elementary School Orthopedic Impairments

Ms. Suzanne Parkman
School
Address
Phone and e-mail

Dear Mr. Hamal:

While at the library, I picked up a wonderful brochure that I think you will find useful as you look for a summer program or camp experience for Miranda, which I have attached it to this letter. Feel free to keep it, as I have another copy.

You will notice that the first section of the brochure contains a survey-type form for you to fill out to make note of Miranda's special needs and interests. The second part of the brochure has a checklist that you can use as you investigate and evaluate specific programs that would be the best match for Miranda. I was especially pleased to see the section that focuses on physical accessibility to the facility and modifications to activities for participants who use wheelchairs, as Miranda does.

I am also including a handout prepared by our school district's Parent Mentor that lists many summer opportunities available in the immediate area, along with "reviews" from local parents whose children have attended each program or camp. These statements are very helpful, as they are detailed and explain both the pros and cons of their experience. Some of the parents even include their e-mail addresses in case you would like further information.

I know how much care and effort you put into finding just the right community resources for Miranda, and I hope these materials will be helpful to you.

Sincerely,

Suzanne Parkman

Figure 5.24   Print Resource Letter—High School Intellectual Disabilities

Mrs. Judy Marcella
School
Address
Phone and e-mail

Dear Ms. Hutchinson:

Self-Determination (SD) is a topic of importance to students with disabilities and their families, and, as you know, we have been working on teaching our students to acquire such skills as making choices, setting goals, asking questions, and being assertive in appropriate ways.

For your information, I've attached a recent article from the journal *Teaching Exceptional Children* titled "Why Is This Cake on Fire? Inviting Students Into the IEP Process" that describes some of the components of SD training and its positive effects on students' active participation in IEP meetings.

Carly, although only a freshman, has been doing very well in many of the components of our SD training program. One way that you could give her even more practice in these skills at home would be to have periodic family meetings (to plan weekend activities or assign chores to your children) that would follow the "The Self-Directed IEP Leadership Steps" format described in the article. Giving Carly practice in executing these 12 steps will serve her well not only in IEP meetings but in social and vocational situations as well.

Thanks for your continued support for our program. Please feel free to visit our class when we are working on one of our SD training modules, and call me if you have any questions.

Sincerely,

Judy Marcella

Figure 5.25   Print Resource Letter—Middle School Orthopedic Impairments

Ms. Anna Bayert
School
Address
Phone and e-mail

Dear Mr. and Mrs. Smith:

Recently, you asked me about possibly obtaining a stander for Susie to use at home. I have spoken with the physical therapist who works with Susie here at school, and we both agree that a home stander would benefit Susie greatly. Currently Susie is in her wheelchair the majority of the school day, but she does get out for three twenty-minute periods each day when she is either lying on a mat or placed in a stander while working with one of the classroom aides. I think that having a stander at home would allow her brief periods of time to participate in activities that take place on a raised surface with her sisters and family.

Choosing a stander is a big decision, and I have been doing some research to assist you. I came across a wonderful article in *Exceptional Parent* magazine on standers titled "Standing Tall: The Benefits of Standing Devices." The article is written by a physical therapist and provides a lot of in-depth information while remaining very readable. The article gives advice on finding a vendor who will work with you and Susie and keep your best interests in mind.

The article also describes the different kinds of standers. There are several types to choose from, and this article can help you, in collaboration with Susie's physical therapist, figure out which one would work best for Susie. The article also lists several benefits that standers can provide for individuals. There is even advice on figuring out funding once a stander has been chosen.

I have attached a copy of this article to this letter. I hope that this information helps you begin your search. Susie's physical therapist and I will be more than happy to assist you. If you have any questions, please feel free to contact me by either phone or e-mail.

Sincerely,

Ms. Bayert

SOURCE: Contributed by Anna Bayert.

Figure 5.26   Print Resource Letter—High School Severe Disabilities

Mrs. Gretchen Gossett
School
Address
Phone and e-mail

Dear Mrs. Laughlin:

I came across the attached article titled "Independent Living Skills Can Be Fun!" in a recent issue of *Exceptional Parent* magazine and wanted to share it with you. In our recent conversation, you mentioned that you couldn't find an informal, community-based daily living skills experience for Bethany during the summer. This article summarizes what one mother did in a similar situation.

The author explains how she and some other parents set up the program for independent daily living skills. She discusses how they arranged for a facilitator, counselors, finances, and social activities. Her summary includes testimony from some of the girls who shared how much they enjoyed it and learned from participating.

The author also explains what she thought could have been done better and what she thought they had done well. I believe the lessons that this author learned could become a foundation for you in instituting a similar program for Bethany and some of her friends or classmates.

One of the main benefits of this program that would apply to Bethany is the fact that someone other than her mother will teach these important daily living skills, and she will be learning them in a social context with friends. For example, Bethany could learn to shop for an appropriate outfit by actually buying the outfit with some friends (and the facilitator, of course).

I have had a few other parents inquire about teaching their daughters independent living skills during the summer. If after reading this article you feel that this is something you would be willing to try, I would like your permission to give your contact information to these other parents.

I hope this article is helpful to you, and I look forward to discussing any ideas that come from it. Please contact me with questions or comments.

Sincerely,

Gretchen Gossett

SOURCE: Contributed by Gretchen Gossett.

STRATEGY 11: INTERNET RESOURCE LETTER

Try this experiment: Perform an Internet search for the term *special education*. How many hits did you get? Do the same for *autism, assistive technology, homework, spelling, algebra, visual impairments, learning disabilities,* or any other term in which you are interested.

Here are my results that indicate the number of sites matching each search item:

Special education: 55,300,00

Autism: 47,600,000 (Interesting fact: the term *autism* made Google's 2006 top ten search list—in eighth place behind Hurricane Katrina, cancer, and Paris Hilton, among others)

Assistive technology: 27,000,000

Homework: 110,000,000

Spelling practice: 68,500

Algebra: 88,200,000

Visual impairments: 2,910,000

Learning disabilities: 95,000,000

Pretty astounding, don't you think? There's a phenomenal amount of educational material available in cyberspace. But how much of the content is relevant, and how much is not? What's reliable and what isn't? What's worthwhile, and what's a waste of time? Which Web sites are the gems, and which ones are just trying to sell a product, are downright fraudulent, or worse yet, are potentially harmful to the unsuspecting consumer? How do you begin to sort through all this stuff before referring it to parents?

If it's hard for professionals to sort the wheat from the chaff, consider the parents' challenge. It may be difficult for parents to determine what Internet-based information might be most appropriate and useful to them and their children. They may not have the time or stamina to search through the daunting array of resources available. And we know that sometimes parents of children with cognitive or physical disabilities are willing to try *anything* to help their child and may hopefully but incautiously accept the latest fad treatment or enticingly presented suggestion they come upon without sufficient supporting evidence for its effectiveness. You can alert parents to helpful and reliable online information geared specifically to their individual situation and help them avoid online misinformation by periodically sending them a personalized Internet resource letter listing recommended and helpful Web sites.

A Web site evaluation tool, checklist, or set of guidelines, many of which are available on the Internet (use the search term "Web site evaluation" to find many excellent examples, several of which are listed in the References), can help you screen and rate Web sites that address the needs of a particular family and student. I usually prefer to use checklists devised by school, college, or university personnel, often library staff, so I check for the .edu suffix on the URL of sites that come up on my search.

Most of these tools suggest considering the following questions when evaluating Web documents:

1. How accurate is the information presented on the Web site?

2. Does the author or sponsoring organization have legitimate credentials to provide this information?

3. Is the Web site trying to sell something? (This is not necessarily a reason to automatically disregard a Web site—it's just something to keep in mind. Some Web sites with the .com suffix provide very useful and credible information without requiring any purchases.)

4. Is the information presented in an objective manner?

5. Is the information up to date?

6. Is the information covered in adequate depth? Conversely, is it too complicated or technical?

7. Is the information easily readable?

8. Is it easy to navigate around the Web site?

A systematic evaluation tool or a set of questions such as the ones previously listed, guided by your skills as a teacher and knowledge of the needs of a particular family and student, equips you to provide sound recommendations to parents about online materials. Your professional judgment, initiated during your formal academic training and honed by your practical experience with students with special needs, will be invaluable as you sort through Web sites and select the best ones to refer to parents.

Of course, some parents may not have a home computer or access to one (although many community libraries have computers for public use). In cases where parents cannot get online, you can print out all the relevant information from a Web site to include with the letter.

Internet Resource Letter Review Checklist

- ☐ Determine a parent's need for information in a particular area.
- ☐ Identify several relevant Web sites.
- ☐ Evaluate the usefulness and credibility of these Web sites.
- ☐ Select the most appropriate Web site to recommend.
- ☐ Write an introductory explanation for the parent.
- ☐ Describe the Web site and its potential usefulness to the parent.
- ☐ Write a closing for your letter.
- ☐ Attach a copy of the home page of the Web site, or an entire printout for parents without computer access.

Sample Materials

Each Internet resource letter (Figures 5.27–5.30) explains why a Web site will be of special interest to a particular parent, states the Web site's address and title, includes a brief summary of the Web site's contents, and has a printout of the home page attached (not shown in the samples). These personalized introductions to a Web site will likely motivate parents to visit it. The parents addressed in these sample letters have children with hearing impairments, multiple disabilities, visual impairments, and Asperger syndrome. Two of the recommended Web sites have .com suffixes, but they both provide excellent resources, both free and for purchase.

The topics in these letters range from sign language materials for a child care provider, to social stories for a child with autism, to resources for teenagers who are blind, to a book club for a teenager with Asperger syndrome.

Figure 5.27   Internet Resource Letter—Prekindergarten Hearing Impairments

Ms. Sheri Daniels
School
Address
Phone and e-mail

Dear Barb and Al:

When we spoke last week, you mentioned that you were a bit frustrated because Molly's afterschool care provider knows only a few signs—a situation that certainly hinders interaction with your daughter.

Well, I have found a Web site that sells a variety of basic sign language books, games, flashcards, and other materials that look like they would be very useful to your provider not only to help her communicate better with Molly but also to allow her to teach some signs to the other hearing preschoolers in her care.

The Web site is http://www.sandralreading.com/hearing_impaired_sign_language.htm. Most of the materials are inexpensive (less than $10) and appear to be geared to a young age level. With the holidays coming up, one of these items might make a perfect gift. I'm thinking that Molly's brothers and sister might enjoy using some of these materials at home as well.

Molly is a delight to have in my class. She is very sociable and interacts well with her peers, both those with and those without hearing impairments. She always takes care of her belongings and cleans up after herself without reminders—truly an accomplishment for a three-and-a half-year-old!

Please keep in touch as we continue through the school year.

Best regards,

Sheri Daniels

Figure 5.28   Internet Resource Letter—Elementary School Emotional or Behavioral
Disorders

Monica Tate
School
Address
Phone and e-mail

Dear Mr. and Mrs. Sulla:

As you know, we've been working with Diana on a variety of social skills this year at school, and she's been making great progress in most areas. For example, she greets her classmates and me every morning cheerfully and without prompting, interacts appropriately in unstructured outdoor games during recess, and takes her turn and is polite in the lunch line. The social stories we've been using with Diana at school have been effective in helping her anticipate these and other situations that cause her distress. Verbally rehearsing appropriate reactions to these situations has made them considerably less stressful, and Diana is much more relaxed and confident.

Two areas that I'm still concerned about are Diana's negative reactions when I (or any adult in the room) talk to or work with other students in her presence, and her interrupting me and others to get our attention rather than just waiting patiently for a break in the conversation. I'm working with her at school, and I'm hoping that you can work with Diana at home so that she will get extra practice in successfully handling these situations.

To help you do this, I've found a very useful Web site that has a variety of brief social stories that address these types of situations and would be helpful for you to read and review with Diana several times a week. The URL is http://www.polyxo.com/. You'll find these social stories under the "At Home" and "Being Polite" sections. The site also gives some interesting background information about social stories and how to implement them most effectively. Although this is a .com Web site, these stories are available free of charge.

If I find any additional sources for social stories I will send them along to you. Please feel free to call me if you have any questions or suggestions that I could follow up on.

Thanks,

Monica Tate

Figure 5.29 Internet Resource Letter—Middle School Visual Impairments

Mr. Gregory Washington
School
Address
Phone and e-mail

Dear Mr. and Mrs. Papaharis:

During our conferences over the past two years, you've expressed an interest in obtaining additional information to use with and on behalf of Maria. I've found an excellent Web site that is packed with materials that might be useful to you.

The National Federation for the Blind's (NFB) Web site is http://www.nfb.org/nfb/Default.asp. The NFB states that it is the largest membership organization for people who are blind, and it has many objectives, including "advocacy, education, research, technology, and programs encouraging independence and self-confidence."

I think the best feature of the Web site is that it links the user to many great resources in the areas of living, working, learning, and recreation. Many of these resources are applicable to students in the middle school grades. Though all of the information on the site is free of charge, they also have an extensive product catalog that you might want to look over. The Web site is very well organized and user-friendly.

I hope you find this Web site useful, and please let me know if you have any questions.

Best regards,

Greg Washington

Figure 5.30 Internet Resource Letter—High School Autism

Miss Mary Sato
School
Address
Phone and e-mail

Dear Mr. and Mrs. O'Henry:

At our last conference, you expressed a desire for Cory to participate more in age-appropriate leisure time activities. I certainly agree that Cory would enjoy and benefit from more recreational activities, especially those that will spark his interest and bring him into contact with his peers in community settings.

There is a wonderful program called the Next Chapter Book Club (NCBC) that started right here in Columbus, Ohio. In this program, a small group of young (and sometimes older) adults with diverse abilities and disabilities meet weekly at a community site such as a Barnes & Noble or a Target Café to discuss a book, do related activities, and enjoy each other's company. A trained facilitator leads each book club, and the program is individualized so that all club members can participate, regardless of their reading ability. Cory, of course, has very strong reading skills and would probably enjoy reading aloud to the group. Other members may feel more comfortable reading short passages, occasional words, or just listening to others read aloud. Cory would really benefit from the social interaction that this club allows, and he may want to continue his participation in a local book club after graduation this coming June.

Please take a look at the NCBC at www.nextchapterbookclub.org. This Web site explains in more detail how the clubs are run and gives some background information as well. You might be surprised to learn that this innovative idea has had such a positive response that there are now NCBCs in 11 states, and the program has been written about in the *Columbus Dispatch*, *Columbus Monthly*, and *Exceptional Parent* magazine, as well as several professional journals.

You can actually submit an application for Cory online—he is so adept at the computer that he can probably handle this himself with minimal guidance from you. If you would like any assistance from me or have any questions, please let me know—I have worked with this wonderful program before and have some contacts there.

Sincerely,

Mary Sato

STRATEGY 12: E-MAIL COMMUNICATION

I recently received a one-paragraph e-mail message from a college student that contained 11 grammatical, spelling, and punctuation errors. I found it almost impossible to decipher the content of her e-mail when confronted by so many mistakes. In addition, the tone was too casual, as though she were instant-messaging a close friend. Although I am not a stickler for formality, I felt that her extremely informal approach was not appropriate for the situation.

Although this e-mail was an extreme example of a poorly written communication, I often receive work-related e-mail that contains one or more errors. I find it hard not to be distracted by these careless mistakes, especially the misspellings—apparently there's a reason my daughter nicknamed me the "Human Spellchecker"!

But I know I'm not the only one who believes that errors can damage a writer's credibility. Parents who receive e-mails from a teacher that contain errors may start to wonder if the teacher conducts instruction in the same hasty and slipshod fashion. So it makes sense to take the time to use e-mail properly, and the following strategies and guidelines will help you use e-mail in a professional manner as a useful and interactive communication device.

While e-mail may be *your* preferred mode of communication, you'll need to check to see which of your students' parents have regular and easy access to e-mail and if they would like to receive information from you via that channel. Some parents may have e-mail access at work but are not permitted to use their e-mail addresses for personal correspondence. Certainly, e-mail is not a viable form of communication for every parent, and in some districts very few parents have Internet-connected computers at home.

Topics

E-mail can address a wide range of topics. Many special education teachers whom I interviewed said they use e-mail mainly to update parents about students' progress; to ask questions (e.g., "Did Duane do his homework last night?"); to report unusual, special, or positive incidents in a timely manner; and to follow up on requests, such as sending in money or signing a permission slip for a field trip.

Frequency

We all receive piles of junk surface or "snail" mail that we often toss out before reading, and the same thing occurs with e-mail, where a large percentage of messages that make their way into your inbox are advertisements or unwanted spam. It's a good idea to limit the number of e-mail messages you send to parents—perhaps no more than one or two per week in most circumstances—so that parents know that when you do send them e-mail it is personal, important to read, and should be responded to. Sending an e-mail message on a regular basis, such as every Monday afternoon or Friday morning, is a good idea because parents will look for your communication among all the other items in their inbox.

Length

Keep your e-mail messages short and to the point, but take the time to say something positive. As the teachers I interviewed told me time and time again, be sure to communicate something positive to parents at every interaction, even if it takes some doing on your part to find even a single small compliment or kind remark.

Format

As with the dress code allowed in some workplaces, I suggest a business-casual style of writing for e-mail. Although your e-mail does not have to be extremely formal and can have a conversational tone, it should still follow the conventions of good writing—using paragraphs, transitioning from one thought to another, and being free of errors of spelling, punctuation, capitalization, and so on. Sending parents professional-quality e-mail will demonstrate to them that you have put time and effort into communicating with them and will help to enhance your credibility and effectiveness.

E-mail Communication Review Checklist

❑ Use a positive tone—include something positive whenever possible.
❑ Write a complete but concise summary of your message.
❑ Check for correct spelling, grammar, punctuation, and so forth.

Sample Materials

Timeliness of some content is important (as in, e.g., Figures 5.31 and 5.34), and e-mail can be a quick and convenient channel of communication. The content of some of the other four sample e-mail messages is not quite as urgent, but the teachers and parents in these cases have chosen e-mail as their primary means of communication. All of the samples are well written, short and to the point, and have a conversational feel.

Figure 5.31   E-mail Communication—Prekindergarten Special Needs

Mrs. Jones,

First the good news: Melissa looked so cute in her new shirt today. But now the bad news: Melissa's cute new shirt got torn today when she accidentally caught the sleeve on the pencil sharpener handle as she entered the room. She seemed to be OK—the only thing injured was the shirt.

I am so sorry—I know Melissa loves that shirt. I have asked our custodian to relocate the sharpener in another part of the room away from the door so this won't happen again.

Sorry!

Jan Ormand

Figure 5.32   E-mail Communication—Elementary School Learning Disabilities

Dear Chris,

This is just a quick e-mail to follow up on several questions you asked me at our meeting on Monday.

First, Laurice's language therapist has permanently changed the time for her weekly sessions to Monday and Thursday at 11:00 due to some scheduling conflicts. I know you are concerned that Laurice will now have to miss 10 minutes of her resource room time with me on these days, so I wanted to let you know that I have changed my schedule so that Laurice can meet with me at 1:00 on those days so she can be present the full half hour. I have spoken with her third-grade teacher, and your daughter will not be missing anything critical in her inclusion class at that time.

Second, I rechecked my grade book, and Laurice has been doing pretty well with turning in homework; however, she has missed several of the assignments due on the last few Mondays. Please prompt her to get her homework done on the weekend so she starts the week off right.

Last, I wanted to mention that Laurice has been so helpful in welcoming a new student to our class. She has gone out of her way to talk with this child, include her in games at recess, and in general "show her the ropes." I really appreciate her sensitivity and consideration toward her peers.

Feel free to e-mail me if you have any other questions prior to our next scheduled meeting.

Best regards,

Suni Chen

Figure 5.33   E-mail Communication—Middle School Orthopedic Impairments

Mrs. Thomas,

I noticed the last few days that Jamal doesn't seem to be as comfortable and stable as usual when positioned in his wheelchair. Overall, the chair seems to be in good shape, though the right armrest is a tiny bit wobbly.

Perhaps you'd want to check this out with Jamal's doctor or physical therapist to be sure he does not have any physical complaints and that the chair still fits him properly. Jamal's such a great worker and so sociable and pleasant to work with, and I would hate to overlook a problem that might impede his progress and motivation.

Please let me know if you find out any information about this situation that I should be aware of.

Thanks,

Les Taylor

Figure 5.34   E-mail Communication—High School Learning Disabilities/Intellectual
Disabilities

Dear Mrs. Katena,

This is just a quick note to let you know that Damen's homework folder never made it to his backpack before he got on the bus this afternoon, so he won't be able to complete his math and spelling assignments that are due on Monday.

Damen accidentally left the folder on my desk after fifth period when he came in to help me organize my supply cabinet, and I didn't notice it lying there until the end of the day, so I feel that this oversight was partly my fault. He is such a helpful person, and I appreciate the work he's been doing for me once a week during his fifth period study hall.

Damen has been doing such a good job of staying organized this year and is so proud of this achievement, so I don't want him to be upset about this unusual slip-up. Please tell him that I will give him time on Monday during second period to complete the two papers.

Have a great weekend,

Mrs. Markowitz

Figure 5.35 E-mail Communication—High School Special Needs

Dear Sol,

I can't thank you enough for visiting our class today to talk with the students about possible jobs in the hotel and travel industry. I had no idea there were so many and such a variety of opportunities in this growing field, and some of the students have already expressed an interest in exploring shadowing experiences that they could do this year to see if this field might be a good match for their abilities and interests.

Bringing in the photos and brochures was very helpful also in allowing the students to visualize a range of jobsites, and I really appreciate your offer to talk with students one-to-one about where they might fit in best.

Thanks again for providing such an enlightening and lively session.

Sincerely,

Sandy

Figure 5.36 E-mail Communication—Elementary School Severe Disabilities

Hi Melanie:

Well, it was another monumental day for Henry. I am so impressed with the strides he is making. Today he ate lunch without his radio (and it was no problem). Then we went outside for recess with the general education students (on the Big Toy), and he played the entire 45 minutes without his radio—and was playing ball with the other kids. He sat on the blacktop and rolled a ball back and forth with one of his typical peers from second grade, and they both had a great time. We had the radio with us both times "just in case" (especially in the lunchroom where the noise can be overstimulating for him), but Henry didn't seem to mind or even notice that he didn't have it. It is such a big step for him to be less reliant on his radio.

We're going to continue to gradually fade the use of his radio, because he's becoming more and more engaged without it, and he's really making strides socially as well. I know we talked about this earlier, and I think that because Henry needs his radio less, we could go ahead and try to switch what he listens to from time to time. Would you mind sending in another cassette tape (possibly of music Henry might like)? Thanks!

Also, during our music/dancing time this morning, Henry danced with Joan for an entire song. He was grinning the whole time. He stood there, took her hands, and they moved their arms; he'd take a break for a second and then reach for her hands again. It was the first time he really sought out a dancing partner.

He's been *so* pleasant and *so much fun!*

Julie

SOURCE: Contributed by Julie Everhart.

Telephone Communication

STRATEGY 13: PHONE CALL TO AN ORGANIZATION

I have compiled a list of more than 50 local public and private agencies and organizations that provide services to children or adults with disabilities and their families. My current list includes agencies such as United Cerebral Palsy, Down Syndrome Association of Central Ohio, Upper Arlington Therapeutic Recreation Program, Learning Disability Association of Greater Columbus, and the Children's Hospital Child Guidance Centers, among others.

I update the list annually, adding new agencies and deleting those that no longer exist. Parents of children with special needs in a large city such as Columbus, Ohio, are fortunate to have so many options from which to choose. The organizations in your geographic area may not be as abundant (or may be even more so), but careful and persistent research can usually uncover some valuable resources.

The local organizations on my list offer a wide variety of services, such as summer camps, tutoring, support groups, funding for various necessities, weekend group recreation programs, and advocacy and protective services. Some services, such as vocational training and job placement, supported living services, and counseling, may be offered by more than one agency. There's a lot of help available, but each agency has its own purpose, eligibility requirements, programs, and procedures, and it's not always easy to determine who provides what for whom.

Navigating the maze of organizations to find the most helpful ones can be tough for parents. Calling these organizations can be an exercise in patience, often involving unreturned messages, a game of phone tag, and parents' having to recount their child's "story" again and again.

This is an area where you can provide some assistance. In fact, this is a good time to join forces with other special education teachers in your building or district and divide up the task of finding out what is available and useful in order to pool your results and make them available to all parents.

So a few times a year make a phone call to organizations in your community that provide services to children or adults with disabilities and their families. When making each call, ask for and record the following information:

Phone Call to an Organization

❑ Name of the organization
❑ Purpose of the organization
❑ Address, phone number, e-mail, and Web site (if any)
❑ Name of contact person with whom you spoke and his/her position
❑ Services provided to individuals with disabilities and their families
❑ Eligibility for services
❑ Cost of services
❑ Does the organization have any meetings or workshops?
❑ Is literature available? Ask the person to send you these materials.
❑ Comments
❑ Date of your contact with the organization

Use a ring binder to organize the information you have obtained, and keep it in an accessible location so that you and your colleagues can refer parents to specific organizations as needed.

Sample Materials

Sample materials in this section are the results of phone calls to a wide variety of organizations in central Ohio, some of which may have branches or similar counterparts in your community. Organizations included in Figures 6.1 to 6.5 are the Special Needs Program at Worthington Parks and Recreation, the Down Syndrome Association of Central Ohio, Children and Adults with Attention-Deficit/Hyperactivity Disorder (CHADD), Parent PLUS, and the Miracle League of Central Ohio.

STRATEGY 14: PHONE CALLS TO PARENTS

Many of the special education teachers I interviewed said that they always call each parent at least once during the first two weeks of the school year to report something positive about their child and to ask if the parents have any questions or concerns. They also make use of this initial contact to make sure that notes and other communications they have started sending home, often by way of the child, are actually arriving at their intended destination.

These teachers all agreed that initiating a friendly first contact with a phone call can go a long way toward establishing a positive long-term relationship between parents and teachers. These teachers then make it a practice to call parents periodically

Figure 6.1   Phone Call to an Organization—Intellectual Disabilities

Special Needs Programs at Worthington Parks and Recreation

- The purpose of the organization is to provide fitness, recreation, and social activities for residents or employees of the city of Worthington (and the general public) who have special needs.
- The Community Center is located at 345 E. Wilson Bridge Road in Worthington, Ohio. The phone number is 614-436-2743, and information can be found at the Web site, www.worthington.org.
- My contact is Julie, who also referred me to the catalog and offered to send me the most recent edition.
- This spring/summer the Parks and Recreation division is offering "Friday Night Fun" and "Saturday Night Live" as well as six weeks of day camp opportunities. The day camp includes activities such as swimming, outdoor activities, crafts, and weekly field trips. Participants can attend as often during the six weeks as they wish. There is a counselor/camper ratio of 1 to 3, so participants can receive individualized support when necessary. The weekend classes are bimonthly and focus on socializing in the community.
- Individuals between the ages of 13 and 23 may participate in the Friday night class, while the Saturday night class is for those aged 24 and up. The day camp opportunities are offered for ages 8 to 20.
- The cost of the Friday and Saturday night classes is $125. Residents of Worthington are eligible for a discount that makes the cost $100. The day camp is $190 for each week an individual chooses to attend. Again, residents of Worthington are offered a discount, which lowers the cost to $165.
- No meetings or workshops.
- Yes, the information is included in the quarterly Parks and Recreation print catalog and on the Web site.
- The opportunities offered at Worthington Parks and Recreation are wonderful ways for residents of Worthington and the surrounding areas to interact in the community with an adequate level of support if needed.

March 1, 2007

SOURCE: Contributed by Melissa Konicki.

Figure 6.2   Phone Call to an Organization—Intellectual Disabilities

Down Syndrome Association of Central Ohio

- The Down Syndrome Association of Central Ohio's purpose and mission is to ensure individuals with Down syndrome are given the opportunity to achieve their own individual potential.
- The organization's address is 2879 Johnstown Road, Columbus, Ohio 43219. The phone number is 614-342-5757; the organization's Web site is www.DSACO.net. I found two e-mail addresses for the organization: office@dsaco.net and dasco@dsaco.net.
- I spoke with Melissa, who is the organization's office administrator.
- The organization provides many services for persons with Down syndrome and their families, such as dances, picnics, parties, and outings. These affairs are attempts to bring the community together. The organization also sponsors parent and children (according to age) groups. These groups meet to give resources and information to persons with Down syndrome and their families. At times the organization invites families to hear speakers on relevant issues. Along with these supports, the organization has fundraisers to collect money for scholarships for the children with the syndrome and their siblings, for the training groups that are offered, and for their ongoing activities.
- There are no eligibility requirements to be part of the organization. The opportunity to be part of the Down Syndrome Association of Central Ohio is open to anyone in the community; friends of persons with Down syndrome and family members are all welcome.

(Continued)

Figure 6.2 (Continued)

- There is a $15-per-year fee to be a member of the organization. This money helps to fund the programs. However, there is no cost to volunteer or to be a part of various events. One event that interested me was the Buddy Walk that the organization holds to raise money.
- As previously stated, there are group support meetings offered for the members. This organization is also active in legislative programs. Members have the opportunity to attend legislative meetings if desired. The organization has a governing board to represent them during such meetings. The board includes chairpersons and parents.
- The organization is sending me information on its place in the legislative programs, as well as other information about the organization.

March 21, 2007

SOURCE: Contributed by Megan Aikey.

Figure 6.3   Phone Call to an Organization—Attention Deficit/Hyperactivity Disorder

CHADD (Children and Adults With Attention-Deficit/Hyperactivity Disorder)

- Meeting place is the Mifflin Presbyterian Church, 123 Granville Street, Gahanna, Ohio 43230; Columbus CHADD voice message line: 614-528-4141; e-mail: columbuschadd@columbus.rr.com; Web site: http://www.chaddonline.org/chapters/chadd20G.html
- The Columbus CHADD is a satellite for the National CHADD. As a satellite, the Columbus CHADD shares scientifically based research information with the public. It also educates, supports, advocates, and helps to pass legislation that benefits children and adults with attention deficit disorder (ADD) and attention deficit/hyperactivity disorder (ADHD).
- My contact was June, who is a volunteer shift coordinator.
- The Columbus CHADD assists people by finding appropriate resources, finding guest speakers for the quarterly seminars, and providing support groups.
- Children and adults with ADD and ADHD as well as their parents are eligible for services.
- CHADD members pay annual dues and receive benefits based on their membership package. There are three different membership packages. There is the family/adult, educator/student package that costs $45 a year; the professional membership package that costs $100 a year; and the organization/institution package that costs $275 a year. CHADD also offers a scholarship to help members with low incomes pay the membership dues.
- Columbus CHADD offers quarterly seminars with support groups. They also meet quarterly at the Mifflin Presbyterian Church when there are no seminars.
- They provided a variety of helpful materials.
- The National CHADD holds an annual conference with guest speakers from around the country. These speakers include famous actors, singers, scientists, and authors with ADD.
- I found June to be extremely helpful and resourceful. She thoroughly explained things to me about the organization and related topics. June was easy to talk to and had answers to all of my questions. Additionally, she wanted to help me in any way that she could.

March 31, 2006

SOURCE: Contributed by Amy Leek.

(every few weeks or months) during the school year to keep this dialogue going, especially if there is good news to report.

For teachers, the downside of telephone calls to parents is that conversations can sometimes be lengthy, may be difficult to wrap up, and may infringe on your precious time in the evenings when you have your own personal and family demands

Figure 6.4   Phone Call to an Organization—Intellectual Disabilities

Parent PLUS, Franklin County Board of MR/DD

- The purpose of this organization to help parents with mental retardation or developmental disabilities learn positive and effective parenting skills and retain custody of their children who are age six or under and may also have disabilities.
- 2879 Johnstown Rd., Columbus, Ohio, 43219; phone: 342-5807; no e-mail; Web site: http://www.fcbmrdd.org.
- I spoke with the assistant coordinator, Chris.
- Parenting classes and other assistance in the home is provided as needed. Parenting classes last for 12 weeks and cover 12 different topics. Once the 12-week period is over, Parent PLUS connects with other agencies to see what type of help they can get for each family. Child care is provided, and the organization provides home-based programs and case management services.
- To be eligible for this organization, the parent and child have to be diagnosed as having mental retardation or developmental disabilities, or the parent has to have been in a special needs class in high school.
- There is no cost to the parents, as this organization is funded through tax dollars.
- The meetings they offer are described above.
- They sent me a brochure describing the program.

March 5, 2007

SOURCE: Contributed by Tiffany Anderson.

Figure 6.5   Phone Call to an Organization—Special Needs

Miracle League of Central Ohio

- The purpose/mission of this organization is to provide opportunities for children with disabilities to play baseball. They promote the construction of special facilities to meet the special needs of Miracle League players and their families and promote an atmosphere that encourages the entire central Ohio community to participate and enjoy the Miracle League.
- The games are held at Darree Field Park located at 6259 Cosgray Road in Dublin, Ohio. The league also has a nice Web site: www.ohiomiracleleague.org.
- I contacted the league director, David, via his e-mail link on the Web site.
- The league welcomes all children and young adults with disabilities, from 3 to 21 years of age, to participate as players in the league. Other positions are available, including team coaches, who facilitate an environment of fun and participation for their respective teams. Player buddies assist the players during the games. Buddy leaders are responsible for communication with the buddies on each team and ensure that appropriate buddies are assigned to players. And last but not least, the parents assist the teams in planning extracurricular events, bringing snacks to the games, and mentoring the buddies.
- Registration to play in the league is $39, and the application is online and provided through a link on the Web site.
- As stated before, parents set up extracurricular events for the players and buddies, but the league does not sponsor meetings or workshops.

March 15, 2007

SOURCE: Contributed by April Walsh.

to attend to. If you teach at the middle or high school level, you may have a large number of students, hence a large number of calls to make. You may also want parents to know that you are available to speak with them by phone during school hours (let them know the best times to call you during the day) and immediately before and after but that they should call you in the evenings or on weekends only for pressing or emergency situations unless you've previously agreed upon a specific "after hours" call.

Similarly, parents may have trouble taking the time for a phone call in the evenings when things are very hectic, and they too are tired after a long day at work or handling other responsibilities.

Most phone calls to parents should be limited to 10 to 15 minutes. Any issue requiring a substantially longer conversation can best be done in person. Plan for a smooth and efficient call by jotting down the one or two items you want to discuss beforehand. Then follow this format:

Phone Calls to Parents

❏ Explain the reason for your call.
❏ Set limits at the outset, for example, "Do you have 10 minutes (or 15 minutes) to talk?"
❏ Say something positive about the child.
❏ Cover your planned items.
❏ Ask for and listen to the parent's questions or reactions.
❏ Schedule an in-school appointment if necessary.
❏ Thank the parent for his or her time and concern, and say you have enjoyed or appreciated talking with them.
❏ If you have to leave a voice message, leave your name, school, and phone number and suggest a good time to return the call.
❏ Record all of your calls on your parent contact log (see Chapter 2).

By following these guidelines, you will have a better chance of having a focused and successful phone call.

You may find it difficult to conclude a phone call gracefully with some parents. If this problem occurs more than once, you will both be better served by communicating by print, e-mail, or time-limited in-person meetings. For parents from non-English-speaking households, you'll need to arrange for a translator for your call. In addition, some families may not have their own telephone or easy access to one, and you should obtain this information from school records or at an open house at the beginning of the year to determine the best way to contact these parents.

STRATEGY 15: VOICE MAIL

Recording voice mail messages that parents can access at their convenience is a good way to disseminate information about activities or upcoming events of concern to all of your students and their families. If your school provides a voice mailbox service or telephone answering machines for teachers, parents will be able to call you at any time of the day or night to find out such things as projects that are due, tests that are coming up, daily homework assignments, weekly spelling words, upcoming field trips or to leave you a message.

If you choose to use voice mail messages as a way to communicate with parents, be sure to update the message at least once a week, perhaps more often. A parent who hears the same message for two or three weeks will become frustrated and soon stop calling. It's a commitment of time and energy for teachers to record these messages each week, but following a standard script can make the task quick and easy.

Each weekly message should follow this format:

Voice Mail Messages

- ❏ Identify yourself and your class (so parents are sure they have the correct voice mail).
- ❏ State the date—day of the week, month, date, and year.
- ❏ Tell about class activities or news of interest—usually limit the number to three or four items, and don't include information on any individual students, to preserve confidentiality.
- ❏ Speak slowly and clearly so that parents can write down the information if they wish.
- ❏ Suggest that parents leave a message if they have any questions.
- ❏ Be aware that students may call your voice mail too.
- ❏ **Check your voice mail messages daily** in case you need to return calls to parents.

Following these guidelines will allow you to impart information to parents who wish to become informed with a quick, noninteractive phone call. You can use voice mail as one of many strategies in your overall parent involvement action plan (see Chapter 10) to offer another alternative communication opportunity to parents who might find it helpful and handy.

Following are two examples of voice mail messages:

"You have reached the voice mail of Karen Michaels at the Oak Street Middle School. Today is Monday, September 17, 2007.

"First, some reminders. Students in Mr. Gomez's science class have a chapter test on Friday, September 20, and students in Miss Peterson's history class have their Native American project due on Thursday, September 19.

"Parents, please remember to sign up for parent-teacher conferences in two weeks. You can do so by calling or e-mailing me or by stopping by my room to sign up.

"For your information, all of my students are using the new end-of-the-day five-minute check-in stops at my resource room to review the events of the day and to show me that their subject notebooks are organized, that their planners are up to date, and that they have the necessary materials to complete their homework and study for upcoming tests. Please encourage your children to stay on track with the daily check-ins.

"Please leave a message after the tone with any comments or questions or if you would like me to get back to you."

(Continued)

(Continued)

"Hi, it's Friday, March 21, 2008, and this is the voice mailbox of Pete Allen at Rosemont Elementary School.

"It's been a busy week! Our field trip to the Westbury Farm was great, and thanks to all the parents who helped out. Not only did the students have a wonderful time touring the farm and seeing all the animals, but they also learned many new vocabulary words, found out how farm animals are cared for and vegetables planted, and wrote about their experiences.

"Back to the school front. Next week our social studies unit will be on communities. We'll be doing activities that focus on community helpers such as fire fighters, police officers, and librarians and learning what they do and why people choose these careers.

"We have a new adapted physical education (or APE) teacher, Ms. Ford, who is working out a fun exercise program tailored to each student's individual needs. Ms. Ford will be sending each of you the program in the next week so that you can help your child continue to exercise at home. Thanks for calling, leave a message if you wish, and have a nice weekend."

In-Person Meetings

- Parent Group Meetings (Strategy 16)
- Preconference Parent Survey (Strategy 17)
- Tips for Successful Conferences (Strategy 18)

STRATEGY 16: PARENT GROUP MEETINGS

Mrs. Cargill, the mother of a teenaged son with autism, is an active participant in a parent group that is a local chapter of a national autism organization. When I asked her about what benefits she gained from attending the meetings, Mrs. Cargill told me that she found great comfort in spending time with such a supportive group of people who had been through many of the same challenges she had experienced. She also told me that her fellow parents could often provide answers to questions and access to resources that she had not been able to find elsewhere.

Ms. Dennis, whose daughter has both Down syndrome and autism, served as president of a parent group sponsored by her local school district. This group included parents of children with a wide variety of disabilities. However, this parent (whose daughter is now 16) is no longer active in face-to-face parent groups but rather has several online support and information groups in which she regularly participates. Ms. Dennis now finds it more convenient to communicate with other parents in this way.

Some time ago I attended a meeting of a local chapter of a national parent group. It took place in the evening at a central location, and there were about a dozen parents in attendance. I left feeling well informed about several of the agenda issues, but even more significantly, I left with a feeling of deep admiration for the resourceful and resilient people who were in attendance. At the same time, attending this meeting made me realize that although I've worked in the field of special education for many years and have a sincere and long-standing interest in understanding the needs of parents, I will never fully comprehend what it's like to face the problems and have the often lifelong responsibility of having a child with disabilities. It was clear to me that many parents need the opportunity to interact with their peers in groups and one-to-one situations and to gain information and strength from one another.

Parent groups are so important for parents to have access to, though they are certainly not equally helpful or even appropriate for everyone. Parent groups can be especially helpful to parents of children with disabilities at crucial points in their child's life, for example, when first receiving a diagnosis, when starting in-home or center-based early intervention, and at transition points such as middle school to high school, and so forth. For other parents, these groups provide a continuing and supportive resource from the time of their children's birth through their emergence into adulthood. But for others, formal or informal parent groups are just not their cup of tea, and they seek support from other sources such as family, friends, or the Internet.

Some parent groups continue for many years, and some come and go, with new ones appearing on the scene to take their place, especially in populous areas. Sometimes it can be hard for parents to keep track of which parent groups are active, which have regular or occasional meetings, which have libraries and resource people available, and which perform functions such as legal assistance or advocacy. You can help parents find out about parent groups by attending a local parent group meeting (e.g., CHADD, ARC, sensory impairments, as well as noncategorical special education parent groups) once a year and recording information about what resources and services are offered by each particular group. As suggested in Chapter 6 in the Phone Call to an Organization section, you can partner with other special educators in your building or district to perform this task and pool the results of your findings in a notebook conveniently available to all parents.

You'll want to make sure you record the following information for each parent group meeting you attend:

Parent Group Meeting

❏ Name of parent group
❏ Brief description and purpose/goals of the group
❏ Sponsoring organization (including address, phone number, e-mail address, and Web site, if any)
❏ Meeting location, date, and time
❏ Agenda/topics covered
❏ Summary of meeting, including your reactions
❏ Information on how to join the group, including cost, if any
❏ Schedule of future meetings
❏ Collect any brochures or handouts you obtained at the meeting.

Attending a local parent group meeting will provide you with additional resources to share with your parents and provide more opportunities for them to get involved if they so desire.

Sample Materials

The four examples in Figures 7.1–7.4 describe a varied set of parent groups and represent unique entities as well as local chapters of national organizations. These groups include Families United, Autism Society/Central Ohio Chapter, CP Parents Columbus, and Parents and Guardians of Autistic Children.

Figure 7.1 Parent Group Meeting—Intellectual Disabilities

Families United

- This organization provides informational meetings and support for families who have a member with mental retardation or other disabilities.
- The Overbrook Presbyterian Church sponsors the group.
- The address of the church is 4131 North High Street, Columbus, Ohio 43214, and the phone number is 268-5277. The meeting I attended was held on Thursday, April 13, 2006, from 7 P.M. to 9 P.M.
- The agenda for this meeting included a guest speaker, Ann, a psychologist who provides workshops to individuals with mental retardation, on the topics of death, dying, and loss. Ann explained that the curriculum she uses includes topics such as how to explain the life cycle and concepts of death, including the causes of death, the permanence of death, and grief. The workshops also include role-playing appropriate behavior at calling hours and funerals. She concluded with how important it is for each person to make his or her wishes known regarding type of funeral, style of dress, and so on. It was a sad topic, but a necessary one.
- Once Ann completed her presentation, one of the parents mentioned that she and her husband had recently planned and paid for their funerals as well as their son's but that after this meeting she was going to consult with her son to see how he wanted his funeral formatted. Another woman mentioned that an uncle had died in the middle of the night and that she had awakened her son (who has mental retardation and autism) so that he could say his good-byes and how she had always wondered if she had done the right thing. Ann reassured her that she had, which is being honest at all times.
- A mother told the story of how her son with mental retardation was a pallbearer at his grandfather's funeral and that he had handled everything very well until the casket began lowering into the grave. In retrospect, she realized the importance of explaining every aspect of the funeral before it happens.
- Attend one of the monthly meetings to join.
- This was a very supportive group, and the topic presented at this meeting was informative. Attending the meeting helped me to further understand how much more time and effort parents of children with special needs have to put forth just to accomplish everyday tasks and activities.

SOURCE: Contributed by Gretchen Gossett.

Figure 7.2 Parent Group Meeting—Autism

Autism Society, Central Ohio Chapter

- This organization provides a wide range of education, support, and advocacy services to individuals, parents, and professionals.
- The local sponsoring organization is the Central Ohio Special Education Regional Resource Center (COSERRC) at 470 Glenmont Avenue, Columbus, Ohio 43214; phone is 614-262-4545. You can reach the officers via e-mail links on their Web site: http://www.autism-centralohio.com/.
- The monthly (last Tuesday of the month at 7:00 P.M.) meeting place is the COSERRC, where there is also a resource library.
- I attended the meeting on February 2, 2006, from 7:00 P.M. to 9:00 P.M.
- The agenda included introductions by members and visitors, presentation of the annual chapter finance report, presentations by representatives from Recreation Unlimited, Columbus Parks and Recreation, Habilitation Services Inc., Nisonger Center, as well as information about other agencies that could not send representatives: Helping Hands Center, Jewish Community Center, Talisman Summer Camp, Columbus Speech and Hearing, Oakstone Academy Summer Programs, Step By Step, Worthington Recreation Group, and the Southeast Branch of the Columbus Metropolitan Library.

(Continued)

Figure 7.2 (Continued)

- I went into this meeting thinking that I knew what it would be like because I had attended a number of other support groups with clients in the past. However, I was incorrect in my assumptions. The Autism Society meeting was like a detailed resource seminar for parents and caregivers of children with autism. For the most part, the meeting seemed to target autism-knowledgeable parents. I say this because most of the parents—and the members too—talked about their children's diagnoses using technical terminology. For instance, one mother said that her son was "on the spectrum." Several parents referred to their child's autism diagnosis by abbreviations such as "PDD NOS on the spectrum." Clearly these are parents who are informed, are eager to get more informed, and are finding additional resources for their children.
- I was impressed with the number of representatives from various community agencies and organizations that attended and described their programs in great detail. Each representative brought brochures, business cards, applications, and information for contacting their agency. These representatives really seemed to care about providing the best therapeutic methods and treatments for children with autism. One popular theme appeared to be about summer camp opportunities for children with disabilities, and many of the agencies present at the meeting had a summer camp program.

SOURCE: Contributed by Amy Leek.

Figure 7.3   Parent Group Meeting—Orthopedic Impairments

Cerebral Palsy (CP) Parents Columbus

- This is a group of parents who have children with cerebral palsy. They get together once a month to discuss issues and to share stories. The mission states: "CP Parents Columbus exists to bring individuals and families living with Cerebral Palsy together to share information and resources, personal experiences, advice and support."
- There is no sponsoring organization. They do all of the work on their own, and the group was started by a couple of parents. In the beginning, the Early Childhood Resource Center helped to send out flyers, but that no longer exists.
- The meeting location was the Ronald McDonald House, and the meeting was held March 5, 2007, from 6 P.M. to 8 P.M.
- This meeting featured guest speakers John Martin—new director of the Ohio Department of Mental Retardation and Developmental Disabilities, who has a son with CP—and Peggy Martin—Family Advisory Council. There wasn't a set agenda, but the topics covered included introductions and descriptions of children, surgery decisions, hiring student providers for home care, discussion of the future for a new member whose eleven-month-old son was recently diagnosed, CP advocacy and steps to help raise awareness, the state MRDD budget, IO waiver and waiting lists, and an overview of the Family Advisory Council.
- I felt that the meeting was very informative and would be helpful to a family that has been affected by CP. I enjoyed hearing the stories of the families when they introduced themselves. It seemed to be a comfort to know that there are many others out there in the same situation. The question and answer session with John Martin was very helpful to many of the parents. The meeting was informal, which I felt made everyone more comfortable. The parents offered advice to one another and jumped in when they had a good story or piece of information to share. The members of the group really seemed to get along well.
- Handouts and brochures were available.
- To join CP Parents Columbus you can e-mail Lynne (founder) at lfogel@insight.rr.com. This will also get you on the mailing list. There is no charge; anyone is welcome to come to a meeting at any time.

SOURCE: Contributed by Krista Gavarkavich.

Figure 7.4   Parent Group Meeting—Autism

Parents and Guardians of Autistic Children

- The purpose of this organization is to offer emotional support for parents and other caregivers of children with autism. It is also a place where parents can share ideas with each other. Anthony, a father whose son was diagnosed with autism, started the group.
- This organization is newly formed and currently has no sponsors. The founder, Anthony, is taking responsibility for getting the Web site (www.pgacsupport.org) up and running and for getting information out to people.
- The meeting I attended was on Friday, March 9, 2007, in a community room at 2231 North High Street on the Ohio State University campus. The meeting ran from 7:30 P.M. to 9:00 P.M.
- Attendees were invited to discuss any issues they were experiencing. Topics at this meeting included methods of handling behavior issues, various treatments, school issues, home schooling, and dealing with stress.
- This meeting was a good experience, very informal and relaxed. The environment was comfortable. It was a small, supportive, and intimate group. This was truly a group of parents offering each other support, ideas, and comfort. Several times I heard a parent say, "My child experienced the same thing," or something similar. They offered ideas of what worked for them and where they found helpful information. This seems to be a solid support group, and the parents value the support they get from it.
- There is no cost to join the group; they are very welcoming. There is an opportunity for visitors to the Web site to become a sponsor and to link to the Web site.
- The group meets every other Friday.
- There are no brochures at this time, but Anthony expects to have some created in April. However, there is some information on the Web site.

SOURCE: Contributed by Christina Demetry and Melissa Konicki.

STRATEGY 17: PRECONFERENCE PARENT SURVEY

Before I go to a doctor's appointment I write down the questions I think I might want to ask. That's the only way I can remember to ask all of them later while I'm sitting on the edge of an examining table in a chilly room wearing a skimpy backless paper gown. Like many patients, I often feel exposed, intimidated, worried, or downright scared in this situation. I think that parents of children with disabilities sometimes feel those same emotions when they come to school for an appointment with their child's teacher.

Many parents have told me that they experience pretty high anxiety at these parent-teacher meetings not only because their child is having difficulty learning or behaving appropriately at school but also because they feel in some way responsible for their child's problems, apologetic that they have occurred, and thereby placed in a defensive position. On top of parents' overriding worry and concern about their child, these unsettling emotions can cause parents to forget to raise important issues or to ask key questions at the meeting. They can leave the meeting feeling frustrated that their concerns were not addressed.

Teachers can help to combat this problem by providing parents with a simple preconference parent survey to complete prior to each parent-teacher meeting. The survey may include both open-ended phrases that parents complete to formulate questions, questions for them to respond to, and a space for them to record additional concerns and questions to pose during the meeting.

Parents then bring this completed survey to the meeting and refer to it to make sure that their concerns have been aired and all their questions asked. This preconference parent survey can help parents feel prepared and comfortable and that they have some control of the situation, and as a result, the conference should be more focused and go more smoothly for all concerned.

Preconference Parent Survey Review Checklist

☐ Brainstorm open-ended and complete questions to include on the form.
☐ Sort the questions as to type of meeting (IEP, report card grading period, etc.).
☐ Write an introductory paragraph.
☐ List appropriate questions in fill-in-the-blank format.
☐ Provide space for additional parent-generated concerns or questions.

Sample Materials

The sample preconference parent surveys follow a similar format but, as you will see in the following examples, illustrate how they can be individualized and structured to address a variety of areas of parental concern and to match the student's academic, functional, and behavioral curricular areas.

Figure 7.5 illustrates a generic survey form that can be used at any grade level. It not only opens conversation about the student's past and current performance but also provides a bridge to exploring future issues. Figure 7.6 is used by a teacher of students with severe and multiple disabilities before her conferences with parents. Ms. Henry, a teacher of elementary school students with mild to moderate intellectual disabilities, uses a survey (Figure 7.7) that includes a question to open up a discussion about future planning.

STRATEGY 18: TIPS FOR SUCCESSFUL CONFERENCES

The conference with my daughter's fourth-grade teacher is scheduled for 7:10 P.M. I arrive at 7:05 and stand outside the closed classroom door. I'm tired from a long day at work, but I'm standing because there are no chairs in the hallway. There's also no place to hang my coat, so it's slung over my shoulder. It sure is hot in this school! No water fountain in sight.

There's a nice display of the students' artwork on the bulletin board outside the classroom. I admire it for a minute or two and then look around for some samples of student writings or math papers, copies of textbooks, posters, brochures, class-in-action photos, magazines, or anything to read, but as there are none I stare at the doorknob and mentally will it to turn.

There is no schedule on the door, so I'm not sure if someone has the time slot before me—I think I've heard voices from within, but I can't check because I don't want to get caught with my ear up against the classroom door. I wait for 15 minutes,

Figure 7.5 Preconference Parent Survey—Prekindergarten to High School Special Needs

Mrs. Anika Jones
School
Address
Phone and e-mail

Dear Parent:

In order to make the best use of time during our upcoming parent-teacher conferences, please take a few minutes to jot down any comments, questions, or suggestions you have in response to the following prompts and bring this form with you to the conference.

1. Since our last conference, I have been most pleased about
2. Since our last conference, I have been most concerned about
3. I would like more information about how my son or daughter is doing in school in the area(s) of
4. I would like information about future skills, activities, or projects in the area(s) of
5. It would be helpful if I could also meet with
6. I would like more information on working at home with my son or daughter in the areas of
7. I would like more information about the following topics:
8. Other comments, questions, or suggestions I want to discuss:

Looking forward to seeing you on _____.

Anika Jones

Figure 7.6   Preconference Parent Survey—Middle School Severe Disabilities

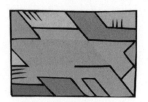

Mrs. Glenda Crawford
School
Address
Phone and e-mail

Student name _____   **Homeroom** _____

Directions to Parents: Please complete this survey and bring it to your upcoming parent-teacher conference. Your responses will help your child's teachers so that they can be sure to address your needs and questions during your time together.

1. One question that I have about the school is

2. I have the following concerns or questions about homework:

3. One thing I wonder about my son's/daughter's behavior in school is

4. In the area of basic academic skills (reading, language, math), I would like to know

5. One thing I would like the teachers to know about my son/daughter is

6. I'd like to hear how my son/daughter is doing with

7. I wish I had more information about

8. I could help my son/daughter more if

9. Other questions or comments I have for the teachers are

SOURCE: Contributed by Glenda Crawford.

Figure 7.7 Preconference Parent Survey—Elementary School Intellectual Disabilities

Ms. Christine Henry
School
Address
Phone and e-mail

Student's name _____ Date of completion _____

Name/relationship of person completing this form _____

At this time my child's strengths include:

_____

_____

At this time my child seems to need to learn the following skills:

_____

_____

I would like the staff to do the following to help my child:

_____

_____

I feel that I could do the following to help my child at home:

_____

_____

I would like to share the following information that is important to the general development and performance of my child:

_____

_____

Please list outside interests and activities your child enjoys.

_____

_____

_____

Thank you.

SOURCE: Contributed by Christine Henry.

knock on the door, and peek in. The teacher, Mrs. B., is talking with another parent; she looks up and says, "Yes?" I explain that my appointment was at 7:10, and she says, "We're not done yet, so please wait."

Fifteen minutes later the door opens and Mrs. B. ushers out the other parent and summons me in. She motions me to sit on a little chair opposite her big desk. She begins, "I have some concerns about your daughter's writing. This problem has been going on for quite a while. I would have contacted you sooner, but since we have these regularly scheduled conferences, I decided to wait until you came in."

Mrs. B. continues talking for a few minutes about the graduate course she is taking in language arts teaching methods and then, at my request, tries to locate some of my daughter's written products. She finds one sample of her daily journal writing and shows it to me but offers no specific suggestions as to how she and I can work with my daughter to make some improvements. A few more minutes of conversation about her expectations for grade-level written work, and then it's 7:45 and the conference is over. Mrs. B. says she's had a long day and is running late, and I'm back out in the hallway after just about ten minutes in the conference.

Although this is not, fortunately, a typical conference scenario, with so few pluses and so many minuses, perhaps you have attended a parent-teacher conference concerning your own child and experienced one or more of these negative and frustrating features.

Keep this scene in mind as you try to determine what is wrong with this picture and how it can be corrected. What tangible things could Mrs. B. have done before, during, and after the conference to make it a productive and pleasant experience for both participants? Consider the following pointers (adapted from Heward, Dardig, and Rossett, 1979):

Before the Conference

Prior preparation for a conference, whether it's an IEP (or an Individual Family Service Plan [IFSP]) or periodic parent-teacher meeting, is the key to its success. Careful planning will help the conference go smoothly and make the best use of everyone's time.

- Reconfirm the date, time, and location of the meeting by note, e-mail, or phone a few days prior to the conference.
- Send parents any print materials you'd like them to read before the conference along with a preconference parent survey to help them formulate questions before the conference.
- Invite any other staff members who could contribute to attend all or part of the meeting, and be sure to let parents know in advance if additional people will be attending. If the student attends a regular education classroom, it is important for the regular class teacher to attend as well.
- Inform students about the conference, and invite them to participate if appropriate.
- Prepare a one-page conference outline (Figure 7.8) to help you get organized for the conference. Collect a set of work samples, test results, data sheets, photos, and so forth for each student to share with the parents.
- Arrange the physical environment to make parents feel welcome. A waiting area in the hallway should have adult-sized chairs and a table with representative

instructional materials, informative pamphlets, and a few handouts for them to take home. Especially at the elementary school level, parents like to see their children's work and photos of them in action displayed on a bulletin board or in an album.

- Arrange adult-sized chairs at a table inside the meeting room, and be sure to have extra chairs in case additional people attend. Position a clock on your desk so you can keep track of the time without referring to your wristwatch.
- Don't blindside parents with bad news. If you have serious concerns prior to the conference, let parents know beforehand via phone or letter.
- Be sure you know the correct names of the parents/guardians/grandparents, and so on.
- Prepare a suggestion sheet or materials for parents to take home.

During the Conference

- Begin the conference on time. It's a good idea to plan a 5–10 minute gap between conferences in case one runs over a bit. If it looks as if a conference will last significantly longer, schedule another conference with the parents to take place as soon as possible rather than let a long queue of anxious parents build outside your door.
- Welcome parents to your classroom, introduce yourself and any other staff members present, and thank the parents for coming.
- Start the conference on a pleasant note. Parents want to hear something good or encouraging about their child, whether it's a brief compliment or a quick anecdote. Beginning the conference on a positive note demonstrates to parents that you see and value their child as a whole person and not as just a student with a limiting disability or set of problems.
- Proceed with the conference at a steady but not hurried pace, and make eye contact throughout.
- Refer to the conference outline you have prepared.
- Invite the parents to ask questions or make suggestions during the conference, and listen carefully and seriously to their concerns.
- Encourage parents to refer to their preconference parent survey if they have filled one out.
- Write down any tasks you have promised you'd do and record the dates for any future meetings.
- Taking notes on a computer during a parent-teacher conference, though efficient, may actually intimidate or distract parents. Writing notes by hand during the conference may be a better option.

After the Conference

- Take a few minutes to make formal notes on the conference—a computer can be useful for this task, but handwritten notes are fine too. A brief summary will be very helpful for future reference.
- Debrief the student about the conference within a day or two of the meeting, whether he or she has attended or not.
- Complete all agreed-upon tasks.

More Suggestions

Many of the teachers I interviewed shared a variety of helpful tips for implementing successful parent-teacher conferences.

Ms. Trask-Tyler, a middle school teacher of students who have multiple disabilities, has light snacks available for parents and other staff members attending her IEP meetings. Sometimes her students bake a few loaves of banana bread during their cooking class for this purpose. She always has representative work samples for parents to see.

Ms. Musser, a resource room teacher for elementary school students who have learning disabilities, includes students in parent conferences and IEP meetings when possible. She works with her students to fill out a form prior to the conference on which they assess their own progress in each of the academic areas and explain their success or what they need to do to improve and formulate some future goals. The students use this form at the conference to present an overview of their "case." This self-assessment process helps students understand their current situation and encourages them to take responsibility for their own learning.

During the initial IEP conference, which usually involves four or more professionals and can be intimidating to parents, especially to those who may themselves have had negative experiences in school, Ms. Musser makes sure she sits next to the parents and, when necessary, explains or gives examples of technical terminology that she feels the parents may not be familiar with. She says that parents are very appreciative of this informal "translation" process.

In addition to providing student work samples, Mrs. Crawford, a teacher of middle school students who have multiple disabilities, collects some of her instructional materials so she can show parents how she teaches each subject.

Ms. Zeitler, a middle school teacher of students who have mild disabilities, always makes sure to give parents a chance to talk about their concerns and to ask questions. In addition, she employs a technique similar to Ms. Musser's, where she invites students to attend IEP meetings to show and tell about the data collection sheets that students use to track progress on their own academic and social goals.

High school teacher Mr. Andres, who works with students with behavior disorders, takes the time to learn about their families' backgrounds, cultures, and circumstances; establishes a warm relationship; and takes care not to intimidate the parents.

Most of the experienced teachers I interviewed stressed that parent-teacher conferences are just one component of parent-teacher collaboration and should be part of an ongoing process of communication and cooperation that starts on the first day of school.

A final note: Conferences may be preferred modes of contact for parents who do not have good reading skills but who can communicate more effectively orally. And be sure to obtain good translation/interpretation services for parents who do not speak fluent English or who use sign language.

Figure 7.8   Conference Outline—Prekindergarten to High School

Date _____   Time _____

Student's name _____
Parent's name(s) _____
Teacher's name _____
Other staff members present _____

Objectives of conference:

Student's strengths:

Area(s) where improvement is needed:

Questions to ask parents:

Parent's responses/Comments/Questions:

Examples of student's work/Interactions/Data sheets:

Current programs and strategies used by teacher:

Suggestions for parent:

Suggestions from parent:

Follow-up activities:

    Parent:

    Teacher:

Date called for follow-up and outcome:

SOURCE: Adapted from Heward, Dardig, and Rossett, *Working With Parents of Handicapped Children*, 1979.

Helping Parents Teach Their Children at Home

- IEP/IFSP Practice Letter (Strategy 19)
- Home Activity Calendar (Strategy 20)
- Home Response Cards (Strategy 21)
- Make-It-Take-It Workshop (Strategy 22)
- Summer Activities Letter (Strategy 23)

STRATEGY 19: IEP/IFSP PRACTICE LETTER

Some of my fondest memories of interacting with my own children when they were young are when I was teaching them new skills or helping them practice ones they were working on at school. Whether it was teaching them letter names and sounds, practicing math facts, creating a science project, teaching them to jump rope or tie their shoes, I felt a deep sense of satisfaction when my son or daughter made progress, thanks to my parental efforts.

I think all parents want to help their children learn and may intuitively do many of the right things to this end, but parents often welcome specific suggestions from teachers about how to help accelerate their child's educational progress. In addition, parents are their child's first teachers, and, because parents have more access to their children than the 30 or so hours a week that teachers do, they can provide much additional intensive instruction that can significantly increase academic performance.

Many years ago when I was the parent educator of an early intervention program (for children ages three through eight), I found that most of the parents who attended my weekly classes and met with me in their homes to develop and carry out home learning programs were sincerely interested in working with their children, most of whom had significant disabilities and seriously disruptive behaviors.

At that time, before the Individuals with Disabilities Education Act (originally known as PL 94–142) was passed, we didn't have the already established and parent-approved IEP (or IFSP) with its goals and objectives that are now a familiar part of the educational landscape upon which to draw. We had to come up with mutually agreed upon objectives for parents to work on with their children at home. Fortunately it's much easier for today's teacher to use the IEP/IFSP as the foundation upon which to suggest ways for parents to continue their child's home learning that are consistent with state-mandated academic content standards, their school's curriculum, and their teachers' instructional methods.

Parents who implement the teacher's suggestions for skill development and practice can achieve three important outcomes for their child:

First, they can help their child achieve **mastery** of skills more quickly, and to a higher standard of accuracy, fluency, rate, or quality. For example, parents can help their child work on IEP goals to improve reading vocabulary, fluency, and comprehension; learn the parts of American government; or practice algebraic equations.

Second, parents can help their child achieve **maintenance** of skills that they have learned at school; in other words, parents can help their child continue to use the newly acquired skills so they are not lost from their repertoires. For example, parents can help their child continue to demonstrate IEP goals of identifying when and how to call 911, using daily self-care and grooming skills, or making eye contact when conversing with others.

Third, they can help their child achieve **generalization**, which means learning how to use the mastered skills in similar environments, that is, when the conditions are somewhat different from the classroom setting. For example, parents can help their child extend to their natural environments of home and community IEP goals, such as using organizational strategies, handling money, or making a nutritious snack.

Activities based on the IEP/IFSP that you suggest to parents for home implementation will provide consistency and strengthen the connection for the student between their two most important environments—home and school. The payoff for initiating this easy-to-implement strategy will likely be increased student learning and ongoing parent cooperation and satisfaction.

IEP/IFSP practice letters follow a similar pattern. First, each letter identifies its purpose in a positive way so that parents know from the start that they are not being presented with a problem. Second, each letter states the IEP/IFSP goal and a brief rationale for it. Third, each letter suggests three to five activities that the parent can do at home to help the child master, maintain, or generalize the skill. Last, each letter thanks the parents for their cooperation.

IEP/IFSP Practice Letter Review Checklist

❏ Explain the purpose of your letter.
❏ State the student's goal or objective.
❏ List three to five practice activities for this objective that the parents can do with their child at home.
❏ Thank the parents for their cooperation.

Sample Materials

The students' disabilities represented in this set of sample letters (Figures 8.1–8.5) include cerebral palsy, intellectual disabilities, learning disabilities/ADHD, and Asperger syndrome, and their IEP or IFSP skills targeted for practice range from fine motor skills to reading comprehension to social interaction/leisure time to organization to cooking.

Figure 8.1 IFSP Practice Letter—Prekindergarten Orthopedic Impairments

Judy Green
School
Address
Phone and e-mail

Dear Ms. Collins:

At our last conference you mentioned that you were interested in doing some home-based activities that would help Marviqua improve her fine motor skills. Using her fingers to grasp and release properly is so important for your daughter to master so that she can participate fully in all academic tasks that involve writing, leisure time pursuits such as drawing, and self-care skills such as buttoning and brushing her teeth.

This week I met with Mr. Purcell, our occupational therapist, and we came up with several fun and functional things you can do at home to help your daughter practice this very important IFSP goal: *Marviqua will use a two- or three-finger pincer grasp (with both her right and left hands) to pick up and release small items into a designated place.* Some ideas for you to try:

- Let Marviqua pick up a variety of coins and place them into your purse or a piggy bank. Start with a few coins and then add a few more on each successive day you do this activity. Use a hand-over-hand technique to help her get started only if she needs it.
- Have Marviqua help you in the kitchen by sorting silverware into a drawer organizer. Place the washed silverware onto a towel in front of her, and remove the organizer from the drawer if possible so that she has easy access to it. You may want to use plastic forks, knives, and spoons at first that will be lighter and easier for her to handle.
- Marviqua can help you clean the counter or tabletop by picking up items and putting them in a bowl or small trash container placed in front of her.
- She can also put pieces of your jewelry into specific locations in your jewelry box.

Marviqua is such a sweet and helpful girl, and I think she would enjoy these activities especially because they would be helpful to her mom. Thank you so much for your interest in collaborating with me on helping Marviqua achieve her goals.

Sincerely,

Judy Green

Figure 8.2   IEP Practice Letter—Elementary School Learning Disabilities

Ms. Sharon Wells
School
Address
Phone and e-mail

Dear Mr. and Mrs. Anacona:

Josh has made so much progress in the last few weeks on his reading comprehension, and I'm writing you to suggest that you do some additional home activities to keep him practicing this important skill. The textbooks and workbooks that Josh will be using next year in his fifth-grade social studies, language arts, and science subjects are fairly difficult and require that Josh's comprehension be at a high level. We also want to make sure that Josh can read accurately for information and enjoy leisure time reading as well.

Josh's current IEP goal is *Josh will answer who, what, when, where, why, and how (WWWWWH) comprehension questions on fourth-grade level reading materials.* Some home activities that will help him achieve this goal are the following:

- At the public library check out some books each week (the children's librarian can help you select fourth-grade reading level books), and have Josh read you several pages each night. Then ask him a variety of WWWWWH questions.
- Do the same activity above, but this time have Josh ask *you* the WWWWWH questions.
- Select an article from a children's magazine, an Internet source, or even an adult publication that you think Josh might be interested in (Josh loves anything to do with animals and space). Have him read the article, and then ask him WWWWWH questions.
- Have Josh read television program descriptions from *TV Guide* or the newspaper television listings. Again, ask comprehension questions.
- After viewing a movie or television program with your son, ask WWWWWH questions. Although this activity does not actually involve reading, it will help Josh reinforce his understanding of what information WWWWWH questions are seeking.

Please feel free to contact me if you'd like any further suggestions. Thanks for your willingness to work with Josh on this very important skill.

Sincerely,

Sharon Wells

Figure 8.3 IEP Practice Letter—Elementary School Attention Deficit/Hyperactivity Disorder/Emotional or Behavioral Disorders

Mr. Sam Walker
School
Address
Phone and e-mail

Dear Dr. Seares:

Matthew has really started making some friends this year, and it is so rewarding to see him playing so happily and peacefully with his peers during outdoor recess. As winter nears, I'm hoping that he will learn to participate just as cooperatively in some less physically active board and card games that he could enjoy with his friends during indoor recess or at home.

As you know, one of Matthew's most important IEP goals this year is that he *improve his peer inter-action skills (including taking turns, making the appropriate game-related responses, using positive ver-balizations) in structured and unstructured leisure time activities.* Several ways that you could help Matthew continue his progress in this area are the following:

- Set aside a designated time (5 to 15 minutes at first) for Matthew to play a variety of board and card games with his older sister. Some good choices might be Connect 4, UNO, or Go Fish. Be sure he knows how to play each game first so that he doesn't get frustrated. Position yourself close by and give lots of praise and attention as they are playing and after they have finished.

- Try the same strategy the next time he has a friend over, or suggest that he take a favorite game to his friend's house.

- Introduce Matthew to a new board or card game each week so that he doesn't get bored. You can even make a chart or list of games he likes and let him choose a different one each time.

- Please make sure that you incorporate Matthew's setting up and cleaning up the game as part of this activity.

I appreciate all the work you've been doing with Matthew; it certainly has paid off. And thanks again for sending in the cupcakes for our class party last week.

Sincerely,

Sam Walker

Figure 8.4   IEP Practice Letter—Middle School Learning Disabilities

Brian Benjamin
School
Address
Phone and e-mail

Dear Mr. Russell and Ms. Routledge,

As you know, we've been working very hard already this year on Ronny's IEP goal: *Ronny will use a variety of organizational strategies to ensure that she prepares for each class with all books and materials; records her nightly assignments, test dates, and other information; and leaves school each day with all necessary homework materials.*

These skills are so important, especially now that Ronny is in middle school where she changes classes each period and needs to move independently around the school building.

You can help Ronny practice her goal of using organizational strategies at home as well.

- For example, Ronny can work with you to devise an organizational system or chart for placing groceries in the pantry, clothes in her closet, and other personal belongings in her room or bathroom—then she can practice following the guidelines she has set up.
- She can help you sort mail when it arrives each day, help you prepare a weekly grocery list, and check off the items if she accompanies you to the store.
- Perhaps on occasion Ronny can help you follow a recipe and be responsible for getting out all the necessary food and equipment and checking off each step of the recipe as it's completed.
- Ronny can make a weekend to-do list for herself each Friday after school and check off the items as she completes them. It's a good idea to include a specific day and time for her to complete each item on the list.
- In addition, you can work with Ronny to organize her school items and select and lay out her clothes on Sunday evenings so that she gets off to a good and stress-free start every Monday morning.

Practicing organizational strategies at home will help Ronny see how much easier her life will be if she takes the time to carefully plan and carry out her daily activities. I thank you both for all you've done to help Ronny make progress in so many areas.

Best regards,

Brian Benjamin

Figure 8.5   IEP Practice Letter—High School Severe Disabilities

M. Pat Carsonelli
School
Address
Phone and e-mail

Dear June and Charlie:

It's hard to believe that we're nearing the end of the school year and closing in on Taryn's graduation from high school. I've so much enjoyed getting to know her and both of you in the past few years and hope that we can keep in touch in the years to come.

As you know, we've been working on many functional skills this year in anticipation of the students' quest for independence after high school and beyond. One area that we've spent a lot of instructional time on is in the area of cooking. Taryn's IEP goal in this area is to *prepare a simple (fewer than 10-step) snack independently using a picture or illustrated recipe.*

Taryn already has had the experience of preparing a half dozen snacks in our class kitchen and has practiced each one on repeated occasions until she feels comfortable making each snack without supervision. She is very proud of her accomplishments and has expressed a desire to learn more snack recipes that she could try at home.

I have enclosed laminated picture or illustrated recipes for the following snacks: open-face sandwich, nachos, fancy fruit salad, easy mac and cheese, and veggies and dip. Please let Taryn select a recipe and then purchase the necessary ingredients. The first few times you'll need to demonstrate each step and let her help you as much as possible. She can also use a washable marker to check off each step on the recipe card after it's completed. After doing this routine a few times, invite Taryn to do some of the steps entirely by herself. Within a few more practice sessions, Taryn will be able to make the snack independently.

As you begin this home program, feel free to call me if you have any questions. If Taryn wants to bring her snack in to class to eat on the days she stays for an afterschool program, that will be fine.

Thanks, and I hope to see you soon.

Pat

STRATEGY 20: HOME ACTIVITY CALENDAR

When my children were young, I kept a month-at-a-glance calendar on the refrigerator to record all of our family's activities, appointments, and special dates. Any event or reminder that made it to the calendar would usually be accomplished or attended to. Events that weren't recorded on the calendar were often overlooked and missed.

In the hectic homes of many of today's students, it helps to have a system to remind parents about school-related tasks and activities. A calendar is a good way to accomplish this goal. You can provide parents with a monthly home activity calendar with information about school-based academic activities and also include ideas about ongoing and seasonal recreational and leisure time activities available in the community in which parents and their children might like to participate.

I recommend recording three types of information in a standard calendar format:

First, enter information about academic activities and schoolwide events that involve all of your students, such as achievement testing, a new science unit, a field trip, or spelling tests.

Second, add information about any community activities (free or inexpensive ones if possible) that might be of interest to families. When appropriate, you can even include a few suggestions for adaptations and modifications that parents could make ahead of time to maximize their child's participation in the community activity. Make copies of the calendar for all of your students.

Third, you can personalize the general calendars you have created by adding events that pertain to a particular child, for example, "OT at school—send in two favorite pairs of shoes."

Where should the family post their home activity calendar? Just as any real estate agent will tell you that location, location, and location are the three most important determiners of any property's value, deciding where to place the calendar in the home is a very crucial consideration. Because the kitchen is the hub of activity in many homes, the refrigerator is usually a good place to position the calendar. Family rooms or entryways into the home are also good locations because the family's usual traffic patterns take them by these locations often during the course of the day, and they might take the time to glance at the calendar to see if something special has been noted.

Home Activity Calendar Review Checklist

- ❏ Obtain a print or computer-generated monthly calendar.
- ❏ Collect a list of academic activities and schoolwide events.
- ❏ Identify interesting and age-appropriate community events.
- ❏ Enter these items on the master calendar and duplicate it for your class.
- ❏ Identify events/activities that pertain to individual students.
- ❏ Add this individualized information to individual student's calendars.
- ❏ Add a note to the home activity calendar suggesting where to post it.

Sample Materials

The calendar in the Figure 8.6 shows a variety of home activities that preschooler Mark's parents can do with him, especially in the areas of fine and gross motor skills. Middle school student Sophie's family can help her organizational and reading skills by following the suggestions noted on the calendar in Figure 8.7.

Figure 8.6   Home Activity Calendar—Prekindergarten Orthopedic Impairments

Carrie Kohl
School
Address
Phone and e-mail

| September | Calendar for <u>Mark</u> |

Sunday	Monday	Tuesday	Wednesday	Thursday	Friday	Saturday
		1	2 Practice riding trike	3	4 Choose fine-motor activity	5 Story night
6 Practice riding trike	7 Story night	8 Choose fine-motor activity	9	10 Practice riding trike	11 School Book Fair 12:00–2:00 P.M.	12 Story night
13 Choose fine motor activity	14 Story night	15 Practice riding trike	16 School Picture Day	17 Choose fine motor activity	18	19 Practice riding trike Story night
20 Choose fine-motor activity	21 Story night $4.00 due for field trip tomorrow	22 Field trip to Apple Farm—all day	23 Practice riding trike	24 No school (Professional day for teachers)	25 Practice riding trike	26 Neighborhood "Safety Town" 10:00–noon at West City Park Story night
27 Practice riding trike	28 Story night	29 Choose fine-motor activity	30			

Suggestion: Post this calendar on your refrigerator or in Mark's bedroom.

Figure 8.7   Home Activity Calendar—Middle School Learning Disabilities

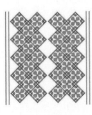

Chris Leong
School
Address
Phone and E-mail

| April | Calendar for <u>Sophie</u> |

Sunday	Monday	Tuesday	Wednesday	Thursday	Friday	Saturday
		1 Math quiz	2	3	4 Spelling test	5
6 Concert at Glenville Library 3:00–4:00 P.M Sophie—organize backpack	7	8 Math quiz	9	10 Make-It-Take-It workshop for parents 6:30–8:30 P.M.	11 Spelling test	12 Nature hike at Perkins Park 1:00–2:30 P.M.
13 Sophie—organize backpack	14	15 Math quiz	16 Social studies book report due	17	18	19 Sophie—practice preparing weekly lunch recipe for family
20 Sophie—organize backpack	21 Bring in old magazines	22 Science project outline due	23	24	25 Spelling test	26 School Garage Sale 9:00–noon—Sophie is volunteering 10:00–11:00 A.M.
27 Sophie—organize backpack	28	29 Math quiz	30			

Suggestion: Post this calendar in the kitchen or in the family room.

STRATEGY 21: HOME RESPONSE CARDS

Growing up in New York City, I've heard my share of jokes involving the sale of the Brooklyn Bridge and interactions with cranky cab drivers, but one old gag always made me not only smile but also think: An out-of-towner needing directions in midtown Manhattan stops a passerby who happens to be a famous violinist and asks him, "Excuse me sir, can you tell me how to get to Carnegie Hall?" The musician's answer: "Sure. Practice, practice, practice."

The age-old adage "practice makes perfect" is true. Just ask any major league baseball player, concert pianist, surgeon, master carpenter, inspirational speaker, or chess champion how they became superior in their fields, and it's very likely they would all attribute their success at least in part to having practiced the fundamental skills of their profession or craft over and over again until they became second nature.

Similarly, students need repeated practice of math, reading, speaking, and writing skills—of all skills, really—to become really good at them. But often students do not get enough practice to become truly proficient, as they wait for a chance to read aloud in round-robin-style reading groups, wait to take a turn at the chalkboard, or wait to be called on in class. Students with cognitive disabilities need many more learning trials than their typically developing peers to master skills, so repeated practice is even more important for them to achieve their instructional goals. In particular, students with special needs who are included in general education classrooms may not get adequate practice to master skills and would certainly benefit from added practice to help them keep up with their typical classmates.

One technique that many teachers use to maximize active practice in the classroom is an instructional strategy using response cards. Response cards are materials given to each student in a class to provide a way for each individual student to respond to *every* question or problem posed by the teacher rather than wait for an infrequent turn. Response cards may be either write-on or preprinted.

Examples of Response Cards

The students in Ms. Dreyfus's third-grade classroom keep a 9" × 12" dry-erase board, marker, and an old washcloth or sock in their desks. Several times a week the students use their boards to practice spelling words, solve division problems, and answer geography questions posed by their teacher. After the students all write the answer on their boards, they hold them up for the teacher to see, correct any errors, then erase them and go on to the next problem.

Mr. Cohen's middle school students use their write-on response cards to practice extracting information presented in line, circle, and bar graphs in his social studies class. This technique allows the students with learning disabilities who are included in his class, who often process information a bit more slowly or are too shy to volunteer, to respond continuously and get feedback on every answer.

Mrs. Fernandez made her own response cards—charts of human body systems (such as respiratory and digestive)—for her high school biology students to practice matching the individual organs and bodily functions to the correct system. Students use poker chips that they place on the correct system to respond to each and every question posed by the teacher. These teacher-made response cards provide an excellent way for students to engage in active practice, although the use of specific cards such as these is limited to one particular instructional unit.

Each of these scenarios illustrates the use of various types of response cards in the classroom. As you can see, response cards provide a means for each student to respond and receive feedback to *every* question the teacher poses, rather than waiting many minutes to take even one turn. With response cards, each student gets intense and relevant practice, practice, practice, even if the class has 10 or 20 or 30 students.

Why Are Response Cards Used in the Classroom?

There is a large research base demonstrating that using response cards in the classroom promotes active student response and improved learning. The reference section of this book lists several excellent research studies and descriptive materials about the use of this technique with diverse age and ability groups and over a range of subject matter.

Many teachers find that there's another benefit to using response cards in addition to a positive impact on learning. Students, and not just those in the prekindergarten–Grade 12 span, enjoy using response cards—these cards help students get involved in learning, and they have a gamelike feel—and students' attention and motivation levels are increased. I use response cards with my undergraduate students in one course where they need to define terms, understand acronyms, and analyze data, and the students tell me they like to use the cards (in this case, dry-erase boards) because they are actively learning and can see their own progress, even in the course of a single class period. The students also tell me that it's fun to use response cards, a welcome change from many of their predominantly lecture-based classes.

Using Home Response Cards

You can help parents use this same active learning strategy in the home environment to give their children practice on important skills.

Perhaps the most common and versatile type of response card is the dry-erase board, which can be used for so many subjects. You can purchase (at most teacher stores) or construct these inexpensive response cards (from showerboard or tileboard purchased at your local hardware store and cut into 9" × 12" pieces) and send one board and an erasable marker home with each of your students, along with directions for its use. Apply brightly colored plastic tape around the edges of each board to create an attractively finished instructional material that parents are likely to use. As this parent involvement strategy does involve the purchase of some materials, you should look into whether there are funds available from your school or PTA to cover or defray the cost.

Then, throughout the school year, you can create and send home lessons in a variety of subject areas that parents can use to help their child practice and master skills using their home response cards. The response cards will help parents structure sessions in the home that provide practice, feedback, and fun.

Home Response Cards Review Checklist

❑ Make or obtain a dry-erase board and a marker for each student to take home.
❑ Explain the rationale for intensive practice of skills in a brief cover letter.
❑ Develop a response card lesson for the parents to use with their child.
❑ Explain how to use the response card learning strategy.
❑ Invite parents to contact you with questions on this strategy.

Sample Materials

Figure 8.8 shows an example of a cover letter to send along with a response card lesson and other materials. Figure 8.9 shows a chart with a variety of home response card lesson topics at various grade levels. The three examples of home response card lessons that follow (Figures 8.10–8.12) target three subjects and skills—telling time, reading graphs, and reading classified ads—and provide a detailed but easy-to-follow teaching sequence for the parent. Data collection is built right into the sequence so that parents can recognize and chart their child's progress.

Figure 8.8   Home Response Card Cover Letter—Prekindergarten to High School

Ms. Hilary Richman
School
Address
E-mail

Dear Parent:

As we discussed at our Open House, the Home Response Card kit I am sending to you today contains a dry-erase board, a marker, an eraser, and a lesson plan for you to follow.

Please read the materials section of the plan and obtain the rest of the materials that should be readily available in your household, or use the additional materials I have included.

Try to complete brief (5–10 minute) sessions at least three to four times a week, because these activities will give your child much needed practice on important skills. Record your child's responses each time on the chart provided so that you can track his or her progress.

Feel free to contact me if you would like any further information.

Sincerely,

Hilary Richman

Figure 8.9 Home Response Card Lesson Topics—Prekindergarten to High School

Subject	Grade Levels	Cue by Parent for Specific Skill	Student's Response on Response Card	Comments
Social situations	PreK–High school	Tell scenarios with appropriate/inappropriate behavior choices.	Mark yes/no or happy/sad face.	Feel free to add your own scenarios.
Math	PreK–High school	Show number pairs and ask which number is more/less.	Write number that is more or less as instructed.	
Reading	Elementary school	Say consonant sound.	Write lowercase letter.	
Math	Elementary or high school	Show analog clock or watch.	Write digital time.	
Math	Elementary school	Show calendar with events recorded; ask what day and time.	Write day and time of event.	
Spelling	Elementary school	Say words aloud.	Write words.	
Social studies	Middle school	Ask questions about functions of three branches of government.	Select correct branch.	
Math	Middle school	Ask questions about line, bar, and pie graphs.	Record requested data.	Calculator optional
Functional math/cooking	Middle school	Show recipe amounts; ask to double or halve.	Write correct amounts.	Calculator optional
Science	High school	Show element names or symbols.	Write symbol or name.	
Functional reading	High school	Show classified ad abbreviations.	Write whole word.	Use ads from real newspaper.

STRATEGY 22: MAKE-IT-TAKE-IT WORKSHOP

When my son was in elementary school, his third-grade teacher invited parents to attend a Make-It-Take-It (MITI) workshop on homework kits. In this two-hour session, we learned how to create an organized kit that contained supplies, equipment, and small rewards such as stickers that would facilitate parents' helping their children with nightly homework assignments in all the key subject areas. The kit was arranged in a basket with a handle that was easily moved to the child's room, the kitchen table, the living room floor, or whatever location would be used. This workshop was one of the most valuable and enlightening times I spent at my child's school. I couldn't wait to try the kit with my son when he got home the next afternoon.

Figure 8.10   Home Response Card Lesson—Elementary School Math

Marty Gray
School
Address
Phone and e-mail

Skill: Math—Telling and Recording Time (accurate to five minutes)

Materials: One or more analog (has hour and minute hands) clocks and/or watches, dry-erase board, marker, eraser

Rationale: Student should be able to read analog timepiece and record digital time for making notations on schedules and calendars, vocational purposes (e.g., sign in and out), arrival time for health appointments, and so on.

Parent Cues, Student Response, Feedback Procedure:
Sequence #1:
Explain to your child why you are going to practice this skill (i.e., state the rationale above in words that he or she will understand).
   Set the analog timepiece(s) to various times (such as 12:35, 8:05, 2:15, 7:55) and ask child to write the digital time on his or her board.
   Immediately check each response for the answer to the nearest five minutes.
   If child is correct, give praise.
   If not, explain and have child correct the answer on his or her board.
   Have child erase his or her answer.
   Repeat the sequence 10 to 20 times and record the percentage of correct independent answers out of the total attempted (e.g., 6/10 = 60% correct) on your chart:

Date	10/15									
Score	60%									

When child has achieved 90% correct on Sequence #1 three times in a row, start on Sequence #2.

Sequence #2:
Explain to your child why you are going to practice this skill (i.e., state the rationale above in words that he or she will understand).
   Set the analog timepiece(s) to various times and identify each time as being morning, afternoon, or evening, and ask him or her to write the correct time plus A.M. or P.M.
   Immediately check the response for the answer to the nearest five minutes and correct choice of A.M. or P.M.
   If child is correct, give praise.
   If not, explain and have child correct the answer on his or her board.
   Have child erase his or her answer.
   Repeat the sequence 10 to 20 times and record the percentage of correct independent answers out of the total attempted (e.g., 16/20 = 80% correct) on your chart:

Date	10/24									
Score	80%									

When your child has achieved 90% correct on Sequence #2 three times in a row, please let me know, and I will give you additional teaching sequences to try at home.

Sustain these activities for 5 to 10 minutes per night, three to five nights a week. Move along at a brisk pace. It is sometimes helpful to set a timer for 5 to 10 minutes to signal the end of the session.

What Is a MITI Workshop?

A MITI workshop is a one and a half to two hour event at school, usually held in the evening, where parents make a useful, attractive item such as a set of flashcards or a game for use in home learning activities. Using these materials helps to increase not only specific student skills but also productive parent-child interactions. Parents—even those with little formal education or training—can work effectively with their children at home if they have appropriate instructional materials and directions for using them properly, and a MITI workshop provides just that.

Participation in a MITI workshop produces motivation; that is, after parents have spent some time creating an instructional material, they are eager to try it out with their child. Another indirect but positive side effect of MITI workshops is that parents will have spent a pleasant evening in your classroom in a nonthreatening situation (as opposed to an often stress-inducing IEP meeting or a conference about a problem) and may be more likely to become involved in school in other ways.

Your MITI Workshop Game Plan

MITI workshops take a great deal of planning on the part of teachers, and for this reason it's unrealistic to plan more than one or two per school year. Planning a MITI workshop with a special or general education colleague or team is a good way to maximize your efforts and serve the parents of students in more than one class, and even meet the needs of parents of typical students. Careful planning is the key to having a workshop that is instructionally useful and smoothly implemented and is a pleasant and constructive experience for all concerned. You can also submit a logically developed and detailed plan to your administrator or the PTA to request funds for necessary materials and refreshments.

The first step in planning a MITI workshop is to select a skill that most, if not all, of your students would benefit from practicing at home with their parents. The skill could be an academic or functional one, based on state academic content standards and/or behaviors targeted in their IEPs. For example, the skill might be doing long division, filling out job applications, reading a bus schedule, learning street signs, tying shoes, recording observation data in a science experiment, or solving social interaction problems with peers in a positive way.

Figure 8.11   Home Response Card Lesson—Middle School Math/Science/Social Studies

Mrs. I. Reeves
School
Address
Phone and e-mail

**Skill: Math/Social Studies/Science—Interpret Data Presented
on Line, Bar, and Pie Graphs**

Materials: Assortment of graphs provided by the teacher, dry-erase board, marker, eraser, calculator; graphs you find in newspaper or magazines

Rationale: Student should be able to read graphs and interpret data, because these are important skills in understanding information in social studies and science texts. Newspapers and magazines often have graphs as well.

Parent Cues, Student Response, Feedback Procedure:
Sequence #1:
Explain to your child why you are going to practice this skill (i.e., state the rationale above in words that he or she will understand).

Select a graph from the ones provided by the teacher. Ask your child questions (there is a list on the back of each graph) about the data presented. For example: What kind of graph is this? What is the title of the graph? What information is shown on the horizontal and vertical axes? How many Americans traveled by airplane in 2005? Was that more or less than in 2003? How many more or less? Which year showed the greatest drop in plane travel from the previous year? Why do you think that is so?

Ask child to write the answer, using a calculator if necessary.
Immediately check each response.
If child is correct, give praise.
If not, explain and have child correct the answer on his or her board.
Have child erase his or her answer.

Repeat the sequence 10 to 20 times and record the percentage of correct independent answers out of the total attempted (e.g., 6/10 = 60% correct) on your chart:

Date	10/15									
Type of graph	Bar									
Score	60%									

When child has achieved 90% correct on Sequence #1 three times in a row for each type of graph, start on Sequence #2.

Sequence #2:
Explain to your child why you are going to practice this skill (i.e., state the rationale above in words that he or she will understand).

Select a graph you have chosen from a newspaper or magazine. Ask questions similar to the ones listed in Sequence #1.

Ask child to write the answer, using a calculator if necessary.
Immediately check the response.
If child is correct, give praise.
If not, explain and have child correct the answer on his or her board.
Have child erase his or her answer.
Repeat the sequence 10 to 20 times and record the percentage of correct independent answers out of the total attempted (e.g., 16/20 = 80% correct) on your chart:

Date	10/24									
Type of graph	Line									
Score	80%									

When your child has achieved 90% correct on Sequence #2 three times in a row for each type of graph, please let me know, and I will give you additional teaching sequences to try at home.

Sustain these activities for 5 to 10 minutes per night, three to five nights a week. Move along at a brisk pace. It is sometimes helpful to set a timer for 5 to 10 minutes to signal the end of the session.

Figure 8.12   Home Response Card Lesson—High School Math/Reading/Community

Carla Padomon
School
Address
Phone and e-mail

Skill: Math—Reading Classified Ads for Apartments—Abbreviations

Materials: Classified ad section of local newspaper, highlighter, dry-erase board, marker, eraser

Rationale: High school students may soon have to look for apartments and should be able to understand the abbreviations used in classified ads so they can be more independent in this activity.

Parent Cues, Student Response, Feedback Procedure:
Sequence #1:
Explain to your child why you are going to practice this skill (i.e., state the rationale above in words that he or she will understand).
   Highlight an abbreviation (e.g., BR, br, BA, ba, appls, A/C, w/, stry, DW, gar, dep, fncd yd, furn, etc.) in the newspaper ads and ask child to write the full word or phrase on his or her board.
   Immediately check each response.

(Continued)

Figure 8.12 (Continued)

If child is correct, give praise.

If not, explain and have child correct the answer on his or her board.

Have child erase his or her answer.

Repeat the sequence 10 to 20 times and record the percentage of correct independent answers out of the total attempted (e.g., 6/10 = 60% correct) on your chart. Also record the abbreviations missed so you will know which terms to review at the next practice session.

Date	10/15										
Score	60%										
Errors	DW, A/C, furn, br										

When child has achieved 90% correct on Sequence #1 three times in a row, start on Sequence #2.

Sequence #2:

Explain to your child why you are going to practice this skill (i.e., state the rationale above in words that he or she will understand).

Write the full word or phrase on a piece of paper and ask him or her to write the abbreviation.

Immediately check the response. Do not be too concerned about spelling errors if the answer is obviously correct.

If child is correct, give praise.

If not, explain and have child correct the answer on his or her board.

Have child erase his or her answer.

Repeat the sequence 10 to 20 times and record the percentage of correct independent answers out of the total attempted (e.g., 16/20 = 80% correct) on your chart. Also record the abbreviations missed so you will know which terms to review at the next practice session.

Date	10/24										
Score	80%										
Errors	Stry, DW, w/, mo.										

When your child has achieved 90% correct on Sequence #2 three times in a row, please let me know, and I will give you additional teaching sequences to try at home.

Sustain these activities for 5 to 10 minutes per night, three to five nights a week. Move along at a brisk pace. It is sometimes helpful to set a timer for 5 to 10 minutes to signal the end of the session.

Another way to identify an objective for a MITI workshop is to survey the parents and have them select or suggest likely topics.

Once you (and your colleagues, if you're collaborating in this effort) have selected a target skill or skills, you can follow these steps to plan your workshop:

- **Title and description:** Choose a clear, short, and catchy title for the workshop and write a brief description of its purpose. You want parents to understand the purpose of the workshop quickly and easily. For example, "Rise and Shine," "Cooking Kit in a Bowl," "Lace, Button, and Zip," or "Math Facts Games."
- **Number of parents:** Plan the workshop for a group of 8 to 12 parents. This is a manageable-sized group for a MITI workshop; too many people participating in a hands-on workshop may cause confusion and, ultimately, frustration if some of the parents aren't able to complete their item before leaving.
- **Instructional material:** Describe, sketch, and make a sample of the instructional material to be constructed that will help teach or practice the skill you have chosen. Remember that one basic instructional material (such as a board game, for example) could meet the needs of a range of students (e.g., by using math flash cards individualized to meet students' varied academic needs). You'll want to be sure that the material can be completed in the workshop time frame, so don't choose a complicated, difficult-to-construct item for this type of session.
- **Budget:** Determine the supplies needed to make the instructional material and their cost. Add an amount to cover the cost of light refreshments. To keep expenses down, you may be able to obtain some free materials (out-of-stock wallpaper samples, carpet squares, outdated calendars, etc.) donated by stores or other sources. Parents may be able to provide materials (such as old magazines or extra kitchen utensils), but be sure to have plenty of backup supplies just in case parents forget to bring in the requested items.
- **Utilization procedures:** Write detailed, step-by-step instructions as to how parents should use the material with their child to practice the target skill. These directions can be written and/or illustrated by simple diagrams or photos and should be included in the handouts.
- **Invitation:** Design an invitation to the workshop. This attractive invitation should include the date, time (both starting and ending), and title of the workshop; its purpose in teaching a target skill; any items the parents are asked to bring; and a way to RSVP (e.g., by e-mail, phone, or returning a tear-off form) by a specific date.
- **Agenda:** Plan the agenda. Start with a welcome and informal introductions of the parents, then get started right away with your opening remarks and explanations, and let parents do their hands-on work on the material. Be sure to allow adequate time for all steps to be completed, and allow for drying time, sharing equipment, and so forth. Precut and prepare as many things ahead of time as is possible. After the items are completed, review and demonstrate the utilization procedures so that parents will know how to use the material properly.
- **Handouts:** Prepare handouts for parents that include a sketch of the item, its purpose, and the step-by-step utilization procedure.

Make-It-Take-It Workshop Review Checklist

☐ Select a target skill(s).
☐ Choose a title and write a brief description of the workshop.
☐ Determine the number of parents to invite.

(Continued)

(Continued)

❏ Create the instructional material to use as a sample.
❏ Determine your budget.
❏ Write the utilization procedure.
❏ Create an attractive invitation.
❏ Write the agenda.
❏ Prepare handouts that include utilization procedure.

Sample Materials

Figure 8.13 illustrates a MITI workshop where parents will create a checklist to help them establish a morning routine to help their child become more efficient and independent. In Figure 8.14, parents will make a binder to organize a set of story charts that they can use with their children to help them understand and identify the main elements and the sequence of events in stories they read together. In Figure 8.15 parents will assemble a cooking kit and a set of recipes to help their son or daughter become more independent in this important life skill. You will notice that two teachers have collaborated to create two of these sample MITI workshops.

STRATEGY 23: SUMMER ACTIVITIES LETTER

The end of a school year is a time to celebrate the many milestones of student learning and of teacher effort, effectiveness, and endurance throughout the school year. It's also a time of anticipation, as students, parents, and teachers alike look forward to the relaxation and change of pace of the summer months.

But every teacher knows that come August or September some progress may have been lost, and the first weeks of school may need to be spent bringing students back up to speed on key skills. This regression, which routinely happens to students with special needs as well as to their typically developing peers, is usually not critical, and students quickly recover and move ahead. But if students' skills deteriorate significantly over the summer, months of valuable school time may be lost while they struggle to recoup their losses before they can begin to move forward.

Extended School Year (ESY) services is one option offered under IDEA 2004 Regulations to keep students with disabilities from falling significantly behind, losing important benchmarks, or redeveloping undesirable behavior patterns during school breaks. However, from what I can gather, the ESY option is infrequently used (only a very small percentage of students qualify, or parents do not often request these services), in part because ESY is not always appealing to parents who may want to give their children a break from school or to involve them in vacation plans or other recreational activities just like their typical peers.

When ESY is not a viable or desirable option or when students are deemed not eligible for it, teachers can assist parents who wish to continue working with their children over the summer. This assistance comes in the form of sending parents a summer activities letter that describes several key activities that parents and their children can do to maintain their skill levels when school is not in session. These activities can be in the academic, social, communication, motor, vocational, and/or daily living skills domains.

Figure 8.13 Make-It-Take-It Workshop Plan—Elementary School Daily Living Skills

1. Select a target skill(s).
   Independently completing self-care skills in the morning, such as brushing teeth, getting dressed, eating breakfast, and so on

2. Choose a title and write a brief description of the workshop.
   Rise and Shine: A workshop for parents to create a morning routine and checklist to help their children get up and prepare to leave for school each morning as independently as possible.

3. Determine the number of parents to invite.
   10 to 12 parents

4. Create the instructional material to use as a sample.

Rise and Shine Morning Routine		
Day: Monday Tuesday Wednesday Thursday Friday		
	Wake up at 7:00 A.M.	YES NO
	Use toilet	YES NO
	Wash hands	YES NO
	Wash face	YES NO

(Continued)

Figure 8.13 (Continued)

	Put on deodorant	YES NO
	Get dressed	YES NO
	Brush hair	YES NO
	Put backpack by door	YES NO
	Eat breakfast	YES NO
	Brush teeth	YES NO
	Wait for bus at 7:45	YES NO

5. Determine budget.

Poster board	$5.00
Stickers for chart	$10.00
Laminating film	(no cost—use school supplies)
Black markers—permanent and washable	$5.00 (parents will each take home a washable marker)
Refreshments (coffee, soda, cookies, fruit)	$20.00
TOTAL	$40.00

6. Write the utilization procedure.
   - Introduce checklist to child—explain how it works and why it will be helpful.
   - Show child laminated chart, how to circle the correct day, check off items, and how to erase it each evening.
   - Post checklist on refrigerator or other convenient place.
   - For several mornings check off items together as child completes each task.
   - Give lots of praise and perhaps a special treat or activity for success.
   - Gradually allow child to complete checklist independently.
   - You may want to set a timer for 45 minutes.

7. Create an attractive invitation.

Ms. Kathy Stevenson
School
Address
Phone and e-mail

Parents: You are Invited to Attend a "Rise and Shine" Workshop

Are mornings a struggle getting your child ready to leave for school?
If so, this workshop may help. You will be creating a morning routine and checklist to help keep your child on task while getting ready for school. Refreshments will be provided.

Date	October 15
Time	6:30–8:30 P.M.
Location	Wingate Elementary School, room 104
Sponsored by	Ms. Kathy Stevenson

RSVP to Ms. Stevenson by October 8 by e-mail or phone
I hope you can attend!

8. Write the agenda.
   - Introduction of parents
   - Explanation of and rationale for routine and checklist
   - Construction of checklists
   - Review utilization procedure
   - Q&A

9. Prepare handouts of utilization procedure (see #6 above).

Figure 8.14　Make-It-Take-It Workshop Plan—Elementary School Reading Comprehension

1. Select a target skill(s).
   Comprehension of the elements of an age-appropriate story (title, author, setting, characters, problem, solution, sequence of events)

2. Choose a title and write a brief description of the workshop.
   Story Chart: Parents will create a ring binder containing 10 reusable fill-in-the blank story charts to help their child understand and identify the key elements and the sequence of events of stories they read together.

3. Determine the number of parents to invite.
   10 to 14 parents

4. Create the instructional material to use as a sample.

Story Chart	
Title	
Author	
Setting	
Characters	
Problem	
Solution	
Events:	
• First	
• Next	
• Next	
• Next	
• Last	
Draw a picture of something you liked in the story.	

5. Determine your budget.

Ring binder for each parent	$25
Poster board (school will supply)	
Laminating film (school will supply)	
Book stickers	$5
Stickers to decorate binder	$10
Washable markers—four colors	$20
Refreshments	$20
TOTAL	$80

6. Write the utilization procedure.
   - Select a variety of storybooks from your home, school, or public library.
   - Read a story with your child.
   - Fill out the chart and discuss each element.
   - Invite your child to draw a picture.
   - Insert chart in ring binder.
   - Continue with the next story.
   - Review previous stories regularly, referring to completed story charts.
   - Once you have completed 10 story charts, erase them, and continue to use.

7. Create an attractive invitation.

Ms. Marcie Mannes
Mr. Adam Brown
School
Address
Phone and e-mail

Attention Parents:
Please join us for "Story Charts," a Make-It-Take-It Workshop, to create a fun way to help your child fully understand the stories you read together.

It will be held on Tuesday, February 6, from 7:00 to 9:00 P.M. at Berkshire Elementary School, room 40.
Please let one of us know via phone, e-mail, or note sent in with your child by February 1 if you can come.

We hope you can attend our workshop.

8. Write the agenda.
   - Introductions
   - Rationale for activity of charting stories
   - Create ring binders with story charts
   - Demonstration of reading a story and filling out story charts—either as group or in pairs
   - Other questions to ask child, for example, describing characters, predicting outcomes, and so on.
   - Q&A

9. Prepare handouts of utilization procedure (see #6 above).

In a summer activities letter, teachers first praise the child's individual progress for the year. Next, they identify a few previously acquired, mastered, and/or emerging skills where it would be especially important for the child to maintain his or her gains until the fall and give a rationale for the parent to actively work on these key areas over the summer. As an additional option, you may wish to add a June/July/August calendar that indicates a schedule that parents could follow to practice various skills with their child during the summer months. Last, the letter suggests a few specific activities or techniques that parents can do to keep their children up and running in the target areas.

Figure 8.15   Make-It-Take-It Workshop Plan—Middle School Cooking

1. Select a target skill(s).
   Learn and practice cooking skills at home, including following a picture recipe, measuring, using common utensils, and cleaning up.

2. Choose a title and write a brief description of the workshop.
   Cooking Kit in a Bowl: Each parent will assemble a bowl of recipes, utensils, and other items to help them do cooking activities with their child at home.

3. Determine the number of parents to invite.
   Eight parents

4. Create the instructional material to use as a sample.

5. Items in kit will include a bowl, spatula, mixing spoon, oven mitt, measuring cup, measuring spoons, kitchen towel, and picture recipe book.

6. Determine your budget.

Plastic sleeves for recipes	$8
Bowls and utensils for each kit	$48
Food and cooking stickers	$20
Refreshments (we will supply baked goods)	$10
TOTAL	$86

7. Write the utilization procedure.
   - Select an accessible place to store the kit.
   - Review recipes with your child and select one to try.
   - Make a shopping list of needed food items.
   - Follow recipe and cook item; allow your child to complete each step as independently as possible and give the least amount of help needed.
   - Choose another recipe the next time.
   - Repeat recipes periodically—each time they will become more familiar to your child.
   - Be sure your child cleans up after each cooking session.

8. Create an attractive invitation.

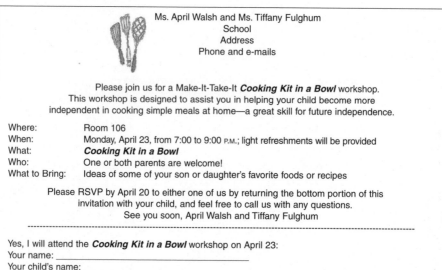

Ms. April Walsh and Ms. Tiffany Fulghum
School
Address
Phone and e-mails

Please join us for a Make-It-Take-It **Cooking Kit in a Bowl** workshop.
This workshop is designed to assist you in helping your child become more independent in cooking simple meals at home—a great skill for future independence.

Where:	Room 106
When:	Monday, April 23, from 7:00 to 9:00 P.M.; light refreshments will be provided
What:	**Cooking Kit in a Bowl**
Who:	One or both parents are welcome!
What to Bring:	Ideas of some of your son or daughter's favorite foods or recipes

Please RSVP by April 20 to either one of us by returning the bottom portion of this invitation with your child, and feel free to call us with any questions.
See you soon, April Walsh and Tiffany Fulghum

Yes, I will attend the **Cooking Kit in a Bowl** workshop on April 23:
Your name: _____
Your child's name: _____

9. Write the agenda.
   - Greetings
   - Overview of workshop
   - Distribute materials
   - Instructions and demo
   - Assembly of recipe binder and kit
   - Review of utilization procedures
   - Q&A

10. Prepare handouts of utilization procedure (see #6 above).

SOURCE: Contributed by April Walsh and Tiffany Fulghum.

These letters should have a positive tone and put forth an attitude of collaboration between the teacher and parent. In some cases, the special education teacher should obtain suggestions from the student's regular class teachers to include in the letter.

Summer Activities Letter Review Checklist

☐ Praise the child's progress for the past year.
☐ Identify several important previously mastered skills and give a rationale for keeping the student proficient in them over the summer.
☐ Suggest several home-based activities to maintain the student's skills over the summer.
☐ Insert the suggested activities into the letter.
☐ Thank the parents in advance for their cooperation.

Sample Materials

The first two sample letters (Figures 8.16 and 8.17) use all-purpose fill-in-the-blank type formats that are easy to use, especially if you have a large number of students. The third sample (Figure 8.18) is an individual letter that required more time for the teacher to compose but is highly specific to the student. Choose the format that would work best for you and your students and their families.

Figure 8.16   Summer Activities Letter—Prekindergarten Special Needs

Mrs. Pamela Meriden
School
Address
Phone and e-mail

Dear Mr. and Mrs. Flynn:

It's been such a fun and exciting year for our four- and five-year-old class. As a teacher I've seen tremendous growth in all areas of development, including cognitive, motor, language, self-care, play, and social skills. Our children with special needs have blended in seamlessly with our typical kids, and it's heartening to see the care and sensitivity exhibited by all the children toward their peers.

Next year some of the children will be in kindergarten, and some will be with us for another year of readiness and enrichment. But regardless of the plans for next fall, I think that all of our students would benefit from continued practice over the summer break on the skills we have targeted during this school year.

If you'd like to provide your child with additional practice in each of the areas above, here are some suggestions of summer activities for Dashawn:

- Cognitive: Counting objects; reading lots of books together and talking about them; practicing letter names and sounds
- Motor: Helping to set the table, sorting silverware into drawers, opening doors and drawers with different kinds of knobs
- Language: Talking and answering questions about your trips to the grocery, library, dentist
- Self-care: Putting on and taking off shoes, putting on T-shirts, brushing teeth, washing hands thoroughly
- Play: Taking turns in all games with you and with friends
- Social: Saying "please" and "thank you," making eye contact when talking to others

Incorporating these activities into your family's usual summer activities will be helpful not only to make sure that your child's gains are maintained but also to help your son use his skills appropriately in settings outside of school.

Have a wonderful summer, and feel free to contact me if you'd like additional suggestions about summer activities.

Sincerely,

Pamela Meriden

Figure 8.17   Summer Activities Letter—Elementary School

Ms. Lynn Heward
School
Address
Phone and e-mail

Dear _____:

I have really enjoyed having your student in my second-grade class at GWA this year. It was an exciting year, and all of the students learned so many new skills that will serve them well next year as third graders.

I am especially proud of _____, because this year

1.

2.

3.

The students in my class showed a huge motivation to read this year. The books in my in-class library have been read countless times. This summer be sure to take some time to read and enjoy lots of library books with your child. Bedtime is a great time to read together, talk about books, and stimulate your child's imagination.

When you have time this summer, if would also be a good idea to practice the following skills so your child will be ready to progress from the first day of third grade:

1.

2.

3.

I hope your whole family has a wonderful summer, and I wish your child good luck in the third grade. Please ask your student to stop by my classroom and see me next fall.

Best wishes to you and your family,

Ms. Lynn Heward

SOURCE: Contributed by Lynn Heward.

Figure 8.18   Summer Activities Letter—High School Severe Disabilities

Del Tyler
School
Address
Phone and e-mail

To the Green-Martin family:

This year has flown by so fast, and it's been such a pleasure for me to see how much Justin has learned in so many areas.

His reading skills have improved to the point where he can easily read the TV listings, recipes, employment applications, and menus, and he enjoys reading some of his car magazines as a leisure-time activity. Justin's work-readiness skills have come along so well, and he is a conscientious worker who finishes all assigned tasks efficiently and well with minimal help. His social skills are very appropriate also, and he can engage in small talk with his peers when appropriate—a skill that will serve him well in a job setting.

In another year Justin will be graduating from high school and transitioning into a job or further formal training. I know he will be a success in whatever path he chooses.

This summer would be a good time for you to allow Justin to practice all of the functional skills he has learned. For example,

- Have Justin look up TV programs for you and other family members.
- Suggest that Justin use the TV listings to highlight programs he would like to watch.
- When you go to local stores, pick up employment applications and have Justin practice filling them out. Talk with him about the job opportunities at these various locations.
- Let Justin prepare lunch and snacks for himself using the recipe book I have sent home.
- Give Justin several chores to do at home on a daily and weekly basis.
- If possible, arrange for social activities with Justin and his friends so he can practice conversation.

I have attached a sample schedule on which I have inserted some of the activities I've suggested above as reminders, but of course feel free to change them around. Perhaps you can work these activities into your summer schedule.

Thanks in advance for your cooperation, have a wonderful summer, and I look forward to seeing you all again in the fall.

Sincerely,

Del Tyler

Sunday—highlight TV listings
Monday—make lunch
Wed/Fri—make snack
Thursday—take out trash
Daily—make bed, clean up room, set table
Saturday or Sunday—activity with peers

Challenges to Parent Involvement

- Conflict Situations (Strategy 24)
- Obstacles to Parent Involvement

STRATEGY 24: CONFLICT SITUATIONS

Parents are usually rational, reasonable, and reassuring, but sometimes they can be troubled, troublesome, and downright trying. During your career, you will probably encounter parents with both sets of characteristics and everything in between. But at one time or another in their interactions with parents most special educators find themselves in a conflict situation with an angry parent.

What Makes Parents Angry/Upset/Concerned/Unsatisfied?

A conflict might arise in one of the following situations: a parent disagrees with a grade you have given; you are concerned that a parent has denied permission for her child to attend a field trip; a parent is upset about a fight that occurred on the playground that he feels could have been prevented; a parent disagrees with your perspective on the student's IEP goals or inclusion activities; the student tells his parents that you don't like him or that you treat him unfairly; and so on.

A parent's anger or unease may result from poor or absent communication, a simple misunderstanding, or a difference of opinion that needs to be worked out. A conflict may be a product of the sometimes different perspectives of teachers and parents. For example, parents are justifiably concerned about the safety of their child, especially a child with a disability who may be more vulnerable than his typical peers. But sometimes this concern can turn into overprotectiveness. A parent who does not want his child to participate in any cooking activities (think knives and hot stoves), to practice shopping in the community (strangers), or to play in any sport (where there is a danger, however slight, of injury) may be angry that you want his child to participate in these activities.

Parents are also concerned with their child's happiness and may become troubled when their child is upset about some of the demands (academic, social, communication, self-care, etc.) that you have placed upon him in school.

Although you share some of these parents' apprehensions, you also want each student to become as self-reliant as possible, so you challenge your students to be independent, acknowledging that there may be some distress and a few minor bumps and bruises along the way.

In addition, you and the parent may have differing expectations for the student—you may feel that the parent has unrealistically high expectations or, conversely, is setting the bar too low.

How to Deal With a Conflict Situation

When you and a parent experience a conflict situation that cannot be resolved by a phone call with an acceptable explanation, it's best to meet with the parent in person if possible. You can do much in a face-to-face conference situation to defuse the parent's anger and to begin to work together toward a reasonable solution.

- Identify the problem by actively listening to the parent's concerns. Give the parent your full attention. Restate the parent's position to show your understanding.
- Regardless of how convinced you are that your position/actions are the correct ones, keep an open mind as you take in the parent's information.
- Explain your perspective on the conflict situation and the reasons behind your actions. Ask the parent if he or she has any questions or can provide additional information.
- Present any additional information and resources if applicable, such as another staff member or some print materials—articles, brochures, and so forth.
- Together with the parent identify possible solutions to the problem and discuss the likely consequences of each one. Be creative, and write down these ideas as you go.
- Consider a compromise—remember to always put the needs of the child first.
- Agree to try a solution.
- Arrange for follow-up and reappraisal on a specific date.

Sometimes it's helpful to use a standardized format to allow teachers to closely examine all factors and both positions in a conflict situation to reach a workable solution. The sample materials at the end of the chapter use the following format for this purpose (see page 155).

For the Future

The best way to prevent unpleasant conflict situations with parents is to be proactive. By using the strategies suggested in this book from the beginning of the school year to facilitate positive ongoing communication and constructive involvement, you will prevent many conflicts from occurring in the first place.

Conflict Situation Analysis Form	
Conflict situation (between parent and teacher)	
Teacher's view	
Parent's view	
Additional resources needed	
Possible solutions	
Targeted solution	
Follow-up plans	
Proactive measures for the future	

Tips From Teachers and Parents

Open communication from the start. Middle school intervention specialist Mrs. Zeitler emphasizes the effectiveness of communicating with parents from the start of the school year. She establishes a positive relationship with each parent with regular e-mail messages and phone calls before any problems arise. This type of open and proactive approach sets the stage for solving any problems in a collegial, rather than adversarial, manner.

Listen to parents. I asked Mrs. Baron-Cody, a mother of two children with disabilities who is employed by a school district as a parent mentor, what she appreciated most in teachers. This parent said she values teachers who really listen and hear what she says and treat her as an adult with no hint of condescension.

Treat parents as partners. Parent Mrs. Naylor emphasized her desire to be treated as part of the team and to be seen as an equal player. Agreeing with this reflection, elementary school resource room teacher Ms. Musser tells parents early on: "We're a team. If we work together, we can make a difference with your child."

Show empathy. Mrs. Crawford finds it helpful to tell the parents of her students that she's also a parent, and although she cannot understand totally what their situation is like, she can certainly empathize with them on certain issues. Teachers who do not have children can show sympathy and caring as well by reassuring words and appropriate body language.

Don't react to a parent's anger with anger. When a parent expresses a concern in an emotional manner, Ms. Musser is careful to first just listen, to then repeat their concern as she understands it, and finally to suggest and discuss some possible solutions.

Sometimes a parent's anger may arise from circumstances completely beyond your control (e.g., marital or financial difficulties). If so, it's a helpful but difficult course of action not to take this anger personally. Remain calm and professional and reopen the lines of communication at a later time when the parent's anger has diminished.

Sample Materials

The following case studies (Figures 9.1–9.4) analyze a variety of conflict situations using the format suggested earlier in this section. Students in these case studies have disabilities ranging from orthopedic to emotional and behavioral disabilities to mild mental retardation with ADD to learning disabilities. The students' grade levels range from prekindergarten to high school.

OBSTACLES TO PARENT INVOLVEMENT

I visited an elementary school in an affluent area that had held a walk-a-thon fundraiser the previous week. The students took turns walking around the school, "earning" money from their family members and friends who sponsored the students for each lap completed. The money was to go to various projects to benefit the school. This single-day event raised almost $20,000!

At another school, a teacher was faced with the problem of telling some parents that she had *too many* offers from them to volunteer at a class party and that all of them would not be needed.

And at a third school, teachers could count on all the parents to make sure their children did their homework every night and to call them if they had any questions about the assignments.

At some schools and for some students, getting parents involved is relatively easy. Parents at these schools may expect—and sometimes demand—to be involved with their child's education. They may offer and be available to expend incredible time, effort, and resources on behalf of their children and their schools. But this desirable situation is not always the case, and many families experience significant obstacles to parent involvement. Some of these obstacles may be overcome or may occur only at certain times, but some are, unfortunately, insurmountable and permanent. Here are some examples of common obstacles:

At one school, a teacher told me that many of the parents of her students weren't able to pay four dollars for their child to go on a field trip to the local science museum. (Fortunately, the PTA was able to provide funding so that these needy students could go on the trip).

At another school with a high rate of families living at or below the poverty level, several parents expressed to a teacher their desire to help at the class party but said they could not get transportation to the school, had other small children at home to care for, or could not take time off their hourly wage jobs to come to school to help out.

At a third school, a teacher of students with severe disabilities recently changed teaching from the elementary to the high school level. When she asked for volunteers to help with several tasks, she was surprised and somewhat disheartened to hear that there were no takers—several parents said they were exhausted and burnt out from so many years of having a child with intense special needs and at this point could do no more beyond the necessities.

Figure 9.1   Conflict Situation Analysis—Prekindergarten Orthopedic Impairments

Conflict Situation Analysis Form	
Description of student	May is a bright four-and-a-half-year-old preschooler who has cerebral palsy and uses a walker.
Conflict situation (between parent and teacher)	May refused to remove her coat and hang it up in the morning when she arrived at school, insisting that the teacher remove it for her. She cried and complained for 20 minutes before taking it off and hanging it up. May tearfully complained to her mother, Mrs. G., about this incident after school. Mrs. G. was upset and called a conference with the teacher.
Parent's view	Mrs. G. does not want May to have to struggle with her coat, as it is often difficult for her to do physical tasks and sometimes very frustrating for her. She wants the teacher or aide to do these tasks for May so that she does not miss out on instructional time or activities with her peers, and she does not want May to start the day in a bad mood because of this.
Teacher's view	The teacher, Mrs. Y., has a set of rules that all of her students, whether physically challenged or not, have to follow. She feels that all of the students, including May, are capable of taking off their coats and hanging them up independently, though some take a little longer to do this task than others. She has seen May take off her coat independently many times. While she does have sympathy for May, Mrs. Y. feels that May is manipulating the situation and starting a pattern of learned helplessness. Mrs. Y. wants her students with orthopedic disabilities to be as independent as possible and blend in with their peers.
Additional resources needed	Mrs. Y. has a clothing catalog for children with physical challenges that has coats and other items with looser fits, easier closures, and so on that she can share with Mrs. G.
Possible solutions	1. Look into purchasing specially designed clothing for May. 2. Both the parent and teacher can work with May on practicing the best way to quickly remove and hang her coat. 3. Put May on a temporary incentive program (sticker chart) for quickly removing her coat and hanging it up at school. 4. Put May on a temporary incentive program (sticker chart) for quickly removing her coat and hanging it up at home. 5. Schedule a brief fun activity for all students first thing in the morning so that May and her peers have motivation to take off their coats quickly and not miss the activity. 6. Ignore May's crying and complaining and pay positive attention to her when she hangs up her coat.
Targeted solution	The parent and teacher agree to try numbers 2, 3, and 6; however, Mrs. G. will practice with May but will continue to help with her coat at home if she gets upset. She doesn't feel the situation is worth getting so emotional about, and she doesn't mind helping her daughter at this age.
Follow-up plans	Schedule a phone call in a week's time to see how May is doing with this task at school. Follow up after that as needed.
Proactive measures for the future	Mrs. Y. will send a class rules list home so that each parent will understand her expectations for the students.
Comments	While it would be good from the teacher's point of view to have consistency in May's two environments, Mrs. Y. is happy with a compromise and hopes that if May is successful at school her mother may be motivated to try the same strategies at home.

Figure 9.2   Conflict Situation Analysis—Elementary School Emotional or Behavioral
Disorders

Conflict Situation Analysis Form	
Description of student	Kevin is a fourth grader with emotional and behavioral disabilities.
Conflict situation (between parent and teacher)	Kevin's science teacher, Mr. A., is not allowing Kevin to go on a class field trip to the local science museum because of repeated problems such as hitting, yelling, refusal to follow directions, failure to complete assignments, and swearing.
Parent's view	Kevin's father, Dr. W., does not want Kevin to miss out on this trip. Kevin is very interested in science, and this trip would mean a lot to him. Dr. W. has spoken with his son, who has promised to exhibit good behavior on the trip. Dr. W. is even willing to go on the trip to be sure Kevin behaves. Dr. W. has scheduled a meeting with Mr. A. to discuss the situation.
Teacher's view	The students in Mr. A.'s science class all had to successfully complete an academic and behavioral program for the month prior to the trip to be eligible to participate. All the students knew exactly what was expected of them, and only two students failed to meet their goals. Kevin failed to meet not only his academic goals, making him unprepared for the trip, but also his behavioral goals, making it a risky proposition to take him out in a public place with the group.
Additional resources needed	Kevin could be included in the meeting.
Possible solutions	1. Dr. W. could take Kevin to the museum on his own. 2. Mr. A. could begin Kevin on another program that will enable him to attend the next science field trip later in the year if he meets the academic and behavioral requirements. 3. Mr. A. could place Kevin on shorter term in-class programs to get him used to meeting academic and behavioral requirements. 4. Kevin could complete some of the science activities he will miss using online resources.
Targeted solution	Mr. A. and Dr. W. agree to try all solutions numbers 1 through 4.
Follow-up plans	For the next two weeks, Mr. A. will communicate with Dr. W. on a daily basis (using e-mail) on Kevin's progress in his academic and behavioral programs.
Proactive measures for the future	Although students were aware of the programs, Mr. A. did not inform the parents about them. In the future, he will do so to enlist their cooperation.
Comments	Mr. A. realized that this conflict was caused in part by his not informing Dr. W. of the situation ahead of time, and he apologized to the parent for this oversight.

Figure 9.3   Conflict Situation Analysis—Middle School Attention Deficit/Hyperactivity Disorder/Intellectual Disabilities

Conflict Situation Analysis Form	
Description of student	Marvin is a 13-year-old seventh grader who has mild intellectual disabilities and ADD.
Conflict situation (between parent and teacher)	Marvin's mother, Sandy, refused to sign a permission slip for Marvin to participate in a food preparation unit that involved several trips into the community for grocery shopping and the use of a range of kitchen appliances and utensils. She sent a note to the teacher that she did not want Marvin to participate in the unit at all. The teacher, Claire, felt that this would be a valuable unit for Marvin and wanted to try to persuade Sandy to reconsider her decision.
Parent's view	Sandy does not want Marvin to travel to the community without her direct supervision, as he tends to wander off. She is also worried that he will talk with strangers, a habit she is trying to break. In addition, Sandy is concerned that Marvin's ADD will cause him to not pay attention during food preparation and possibly burn or cut himself.
Teacher's view	Claire feels that the skills learned in this unit will be very helpful in the long term for Marvin. Marvin has even expressed an interest in food preparation, and Claire feels this might be an eventual career path for him. She is also concerned that Marvin might be embarrassed at being the only student excluded. Claire always provides at least 2:1 supervision on trips and 1:1 when using potentially dangerous equipment. Finally, Claire feels that her students should not be prevented from doing activities of daily living because of minor risks in a closely monitored setting that all students would face.
Additional resources needed	None.
Possible solutions	1. Sandy could observe or accompany the class on the community trips. 2. Sandy could observe or help out in the class on food prep days. 3. Claire could provide plastic knives instead of metal for Marvin and limit his use of appliances to the microwave and blender. 4. Give Marvin intense training at home and at school prior to community trips about staying with the group and not talking to strangers. 5. Give Marvin intense training prior to food prep in the safe use of knives, graters, stoves, microwaves, and so forth either at home or in school.
Targeted solution	Sandy and Claire agreed to numbers 1 and 4 to start and, if these are successful, to continue with numbers 2, 3, and 5.
Follow-up plans	Schedule a meeting after the first community trip to assess its success and decide if they should move forward.
Proactive measures for the future	Claire will provide a better description on the permission slip of safety procedures for all future trips.
Comments	Claire understands the parent's fears and is willing to take it slowly.

Figure 9.4   Conflict Situation Analysis—High School Learning Disabilities

Conflict Situation Analysis Form	
Description of student	Lonnie is in eleventh grade. She has learning disabilities but is included in general education classes for more than 90% of the school day.
Conflict situation (between parent and teacher)	Lonnie's mother has found out that Lonnie has not been completing her homework for several of her classes, participates very little in discussions, and is performing poorly on quizzes and tests. Although this problem has been going on for several weeks, Mrs. Gardner has just found out about it by finding some tests and homework papers in her daughter's room.
Parent's view	Mrs. Gardner is very upset and wants to know why Lonnie's academic support teacher has not informed her of these problems.
Teacher's view	Mrs. Prescott, the academic support teacher, was aware of these problems in only one of Lonnie's classes and was working with her to correct them. She was relying on Lonnie's general education teachers to inform her if there were difficulties, but they had not done so, so she assumed all was well.
Additional resources needed	Information from the general education teachers about Lonnie's recent performance in their classes.
Possible solutions	1. Create and use a weekly progress report for Lonnie to use with each of her teachers to track her performance. This report will be sent home weekly by surface mail. 2. Have Lonnie meet with Mrs. Prescott every Friday afternoon to make sure her notes are complete and in order and to plan her study strategies for each upcoming quiz or test. 3. Mrs. Prescott will call home if Lonnie has a "bad day" in any of her classes. 4. Mrs. Prescott will check to be sure Lonnie has her homework each morning before classes for two weeks, then two or three times a week on a random basis for the next several weeks. 5. Mrs. Prescott will make sure that each of Lonnie's teachers is making the appropriate adaptations for her. 6. Mrs. Gardner will work with her daughter to help her stay organized and on top of her homework and study situations.
Targeted solution	Mrs. Gardner and Mrs. Prescott will implement all of the listed solutions.
Follow-up plans	Schedule a meeting in three weeks to assess their progress.
Proactive measures for the future	Mrs. Prescott will communicate more frequently with Lonnie's other teachers and her mother, including calling Mrs. Gardner when Lonnie has a good day. She realizes that the problem of poor communication could have been avoided and will be more proactive not only for Lonnie but for her other students as well.
Comments	Mrs. Prescott fully understands Mrs. Gardner's concerns and is sorry that she was not on top of the situation sooner.

The following additional scenarios will be familiar to many teachers in both general and special education: Layla's parents are going through a divorce, Javan's mother is caring for her ill and elderly parents, Freddy's dad is in prison, George's parents have limited reading skills, Carmen's parents each work two jobs to make ends meet, Seth's family has moved four times in the past two years, Marta's mother has cognitive disabilities and relies on her own parents to provide care for her and her daughter, Paul's father is a single parent of two children with special needs, Jenny's parents are alcoholics, Bret's family is facing foreclosure on their house, and Tina's mom is 17 years old and trying to complete high school while working part-time.

Fortunately, the problematic situations illustrated earlier are usually the exception rather than the norm. And even despite these obstacles, some parents are able to become involved in some way in their child's education, such as helping with homework, making sure their child is prepared for school, signing permission slips, or attending parent-teacher conferences.

I suggest that teachers of students who have special needs start with the basic assumption that all parents want to be involved with their child's education at some level if they are able to do so. Even parents who do not choose or are not able to become actively involved usually appreciate having information about their child's progress and activities and receiving suggestions that they may follow up on at home.

Sometimes you may be successful in connecting parents to needed resources in order to overcome obstacles such as a lack of child care or transportation, or you may provide just the right opportunity for their involvement. Parents with many difficulties may even surprise you by rising to the occasion and getting involved beyond your expectations.

But a hard and often discouraging reality to face is that, despite your best efforts, you may not be able to get some parents involved. I wish I could suggest an effective strategy that would solve or circumvent this problem, but I can't—the only strategy that may pay off is your persistence in trying to get parents involved throughout the school year. Continue your efforts to communicate and keep providing varied opportunities for involvement by using some of the strategies in this book, and even some parents facing serious obstacles may gradually come around.

10 Staying Organized and Planning for Next Year

- Parent Involvement Portfolio (Strategy 25)
- Parent Involvement Action Plan

STRATEGY 25: PARENT INVOLVEMENT PORTFOLIO

I love television shows with names like *Mission Organization* and *Clean Sweep*, though my husband and kids (packrats all) beat a hasty retreat every time I settle in to watch one of these programs. In these shows a team of efficiency experts helps a person or family sort through their considerable stuff, cull out the nonessential and no longer useful items, and reconfigure their remaining possessions in an attractive and easy-to-access way.

These shows appeal to me because I enjoy making order out of chaos. In addition, I hate to duplicate my efforts or waste time searching for things I have misplaced. I work better and smarter when my surroundings are organized and pleasant to look at. In case you're wondering, I'm not obsessive about organizing my things. I don't arrange my papers in perfectly aligned stacks or line up all my pencils like pickets in a fence. But I do take time to get organized at home and at school so that I know where things are and I can get to them quickly. This small investment of time and energy saves me considerable time, energy, and stress in the long run.

Each year you teach, you acquire new resources to help you, your students, and their families. But if you cannot easily locate these resources your efforts may be wasted, and the perfect resource for a parent may lie hidden beneath a stack of books or papers.

Perhaps you have begun to implement some of the parent involvement strategies explained and illustrated in this book. Now is the time to construct and assemble your parent involvement portfolio to organize your materials so you can easily access them now and in the future. Here's how.

Organizing Your Parent Involvement Portfolio

❑ Purchase a display book or ring binder with 8 1/2" × 11" clear plastic sleeves or pages.

❑ Use the first page as the title page, followed by a table of contents listing parent involvement strategies. For each strategy, insert the items you have produced into the pages. A final section at the end of the portfolio is useful for storing additional miscellaneous materials that you collect.

❑ Add to and update your portfolio each year. You will find that, by organizing your parent communication and involvement materials in a portfolio and using and adapting them to your particular situation each year, you will be able to open and maintain the lines of two-way communication and obtain parents' cooperation without adding significantly to your load of paperwork.

❑ In addition, you will be able to share your parent involvement portfolio with your colleagues, new teachers, and student teachers; to provide documentation of your professional development; and to use as evidence for teaching evaluations such as the PRAXIS III or National Board Certification. And, of course, your students will benefit in many ways from the positive parent-teacher collaboration you have established throughout the school year.

❑ Last, you may want to consider making an electronic portfolio of these materials, though a print copy is often handier to use.

Sample Materials

The covers of three parent involvement portfolios are pictured in Figures 10.1–10.3.

Figure 10.1 Parent Involvement Portfolio—Elementary School

Figure 10.2 Parent Involvement Portfolio—Middle School

Figure 10.3 Parent Involvement Portfolio—High School

PARENT INVOLVEMENT ACTION PLAN

I hope you feel energized and excited about the many possibilities for communicating with parents of students with special needs and for involving them in their children's education.

Perhaps you have already begun using some of the strategies and have your parent involvement portfolio partially filled. Maybe you have used some similar strategies in the past and have adapted or updated them. Perhaps you have identified which additional strategies you are going to use during the next school year. Or maybe you have not had time to get started but are interested in pursuing some of these ideas in the future.

MAKE A PLAN

Whether or not you have gotten started yet, now is the time to make a parent involvement action plan. If you're reading this book over the summer, so much the better, because you may have more time to devote to this important activity. Here's how to begin:

- Decide which of the strategies you would like to implement this school year. Don't try to do too many at once. Select three or four strategies that would be most useful and manageable and choose strategies that do not have to be implemented at the same time. For example, you might begin with the introductory letter that is sent in August or September, the parent volunteer invitation sent in October, the parent appreciation letter sent in November, and the summer activity letter sent in June. These four strategies would be a wonderful start for the first year of your plan without overloading you with multiple simultaneous commitments.
- Set a target completion date for each strategy.
- Fill in the completion date column when you have implemented each strategy.

The following format can be used to outline your plan:

My Parent Involvement Action Plan			
School Year:_____			
Strategy	Target Date(s)	Implementation Date(s)	Comments

Each year, add several more strategies to your repertoire. Document their implementation in your portfolio, and within several years you'll have a wide and comprehensive selection of valuable parent involvement resources upon which to draw and possibly to share with your colleagues.

Good luck in meeting the challenge of making meaningful parent involvement happen in your teaching situation. The time and effort you spend doing this important task will benefit not only parents but also your students. Now get started, one step at a time!

Sample Materials

The samples that follow (Figures 10.4–10.6) illustrate parent involvement action plans created by special educators in their first, fifth, and eighteenth years of teaching. Yes, it gets easier to do more if you stay organized and build on your previous successes.

Figure 10.4   Parent Involvement Action Plan—First-Year Teacher

Teacher: Misty Imperato
2006–2007 School Year

Strategy	Target Date(s)	Implementation Date(s)	Comments
Personal philosophy of parent involvement	July	July 15	
Parent contact log	August	August 30	
Introductory letter	August	August 30	
Parent volunteer invitation	October	October 10	Possibly send a second letter in February.
Parent appreciation letters	November	November 8, 12, 17, 22	Be sure to send at least one letter to each parent.
Summer activities letter	June	June 1	

Figure 10.5   Parent Involvement Action Plan—Fifth-Year Teacher

Teacher: Ken Blake
2006–2007 School Year

Strategy	Target Date(s)	Implementation Date(s)	Comments
Personal philosophy of parent involvement	August		
Parent contact log	August		
Introductory letter	August		
Newsletters	September, December, February, May		
Parent volunteer invitation	October		
Internet and print resource letters	December		
Home activity calendars	October, January, April		
Parent appreciation letter	November		
Summer activities letter	June		

Figure 10.6 Parent Involvement Action Plan—Eighteenth-Year Teacher

Teacher: Mary Beth Post
2008–2009 School Year

Strategy	Target Date(s)	Implementation Date(s)	Comments
Personal philosophy of parent involvement update	August		
Parent contact log	August		
Introductory letter	September		
Newsletters	September, December, February, May		
Weekly progress reports	September–June		
IEP practice letters	October		
Parent volunteer invitation	November		
Home response cards	November and monthly		
Phone call to organization	January and May		
Internet and print resource letters	December and April		
Suggestion box letter	January		
Home activity calendars	October, January, April		
Make-It-Take-It workshops with intervention team teachers	October and February		
Parent appreciation letters	November and March		
Summer activities letters	June		

References

Armendariz, F., & Umbreit, J. (1999). Using active responding to reduce disruptive behavior in a general education classroom. *Journal of Positive Behavior Interventions, 1*, 152–158.

CEC code of ethics and standards for professional practice for special educators. (2003). Reston, VA: Council for Exceptional Children. Retrieved November 17, 2007, from www.cec.sped .org/Content/NavigationMenu/ProfessionalDevelopment/ProfessionalStandards/Red_ book_5th_edition.pdf

Christle, C. A., & Schuster, J. W. (2003). The effects of using response cards on student participation, academic achievement, and on-task behavior during whole-class, math instruction. *Journal of Behavioral Education, 12*, 147–165.

Dardig, J. C. (2005). The McClug monthly magazine and fourteen more practical ways to involve parents. *Teaching Exceptional Children, 38*(2), 46–51.

Epstein, J. (1994). *Five types of parental involvement.* Baltimore, MD: Center on Families, Communities, School, and Children's Learning. Retrieved November 17, 2007, from http://library.adoption.com/Childhood-Learning-and-Education/The-Five-Types-of-Parental-Involvement/article/1006/1.html

Godfrey, S. A., Grisham-Brown, J., Schuster, J. W., & Hemmeter, M. L. (2003). The effects of three techniques on student participation with preschool children with attending problems. *Education and Treatment of Children, 26*, 255–272.

Henderson, A. T., & Berla, N. (1995). *A new generation of evidence: The family is critical to student achievement.* Washington, DC: Center for Law and Education.

Henderson, A. T., & Mapp, K. L. (2002). *A new wave of evidence: The impact of school, family, and community connections on student achievement.* Austin, TX: National Center for Family and Community Connections With Schools/Southwest Educational Development Laboratory.

Heward, W. L. (1994). Three "low-tech" strategies for increasing the frequency of active student response during group instruction. In R. Gardner III, D. M. Sainato, J. O. Cooper, T. E. Heron, W. L. Heward, J. Eshleman, & T. A. Grossi (Eds.), *Behavior analysis in education: Focus on measurably superior instruction* (pp. 283–320). Monterey, CA: Brooks/Cole.

Heward, W. L., Dardig, J. C., & Rossett, A. (1979). *Working with parents of handicapped children.* Columbus, OH: Merrill.

Heward, W. L., Gardner, R., III, Cavanaugh, R. A., Courson, F. H., Grossi, T. A., & Barbetta, P. M. (1996). Everyone participates in this class: Using response cards to increase active student response. *Teaching Exceptional Children, 28*(2), 4–10.

Improving family involvement in special education. (2001, Fall). Arlington, VA: Council for Exceptional Children.

Individuals with disabilities improvement act. (2004). Retrieved November 17, 2007, from www.nichcy.org/reauth/PL108-446.pdf

Lambert, M. C., Cartledge, G., Lo, Y., & Heward, W. L. (2006). Effects of response cards on disruptive behavior and participation by fourth-grade students during math lessons in an urban school. *Journal of Positive Behavioral Interventions, 8*(2), 88–99.

Maheady, L., Michielli-Pendl, J., Mallette, B., & Harper, G. F. (2002). A collaborative research project to improve the performance of a diverse sixth grade science class. *Teacher Education and Special Education, 25*(1), 55–70.

Narayan, J. S., Heward, W. L., Gardner, R., III, Courson, F. H., & Omness, C. (1990). Using response cards to increase student participation in an elementary classroom. *Journal of Applied Behavior Analysis, 23,* 483–490.

Nathan, J. (1996). Building family-school partnerships that work. North Central Regional Educational Laboratory. Retrieved November 17, 2007, from www.ncpie.org/

National Education Association. (2003). Getting involved in your child's education. Retrieved November 17, 2007, from www.nea.org/parents/index.html

National goal #8. (2000). Goals 2000 educate America act—Title I, Part A, Section 102. Retrieved November 17, 2007, from www.ed.gov/legislation/GOALS2000/TheAct/sec102.html

National standards for parent/family involvement programs. (1997). Chicago: National PTA. Retrieved November 17, 2007, from www.pta.org/archive_article_details_ 1118251710359.html

Olin and Uris Libraries. (1998). *Five criteria for evaluating Web pages.* Ithaca, NY: Cornell University. Retrieved November 17, 2007, from www.library.cornell.edu/olinuris/ref/webcrit.html

Parent involvement supports student success. (2005, Fall). *Highlights in special education.* Columbus, OH: Ohio Department of Education. Retrieved November 17, 2007, from www.ode.state.oh.us/GD/Templates/Pages/ODE/ODEDetail.aspx?page=3&TopicRelationID=967&ContentID=5640&Content=32285

Parental involvement. (2001). No child left behind act. Title I, Part A, Subpart 1, Section 1118. Retrieved November 17, 2007, from www.ed.gov/nclb/landing.jhtml

Schrock, K. (2006). Critical evaluation of a Web site: Web sites for use by educators. Retrieved November 17, 2007, from http://school.discovery.com/schrockguide/pdf/evalteacher.pdf

Index